'Fool' Proof Tarot

ANSWER ANY QUESTION USING SIMPLE TECHNIQUES - BOOK 2

ANMARIE UBER

Copyright © 2021 by **Anmarie Uber**

All rights reserved. No part of this publication may be reproduced, distributed or transmitted in any form or by any means, without prior written permission.

Images © Anmarie Uber

Anmarie Uber/Tuggle Publishing

www.anmarieuber.com

Fool Proof Tarot/ Anmarie Uber. -- 1st ed.

❀ Created with Vellum

Contents

Introduction	xi
1. ANSWERING QUESTIONS ON HEALTH	1
Some suggestions for the Quadrants	3
Laying out the Health Spread Exercise	7
End of Chapter Activity	16
2. QUESTIONS ON LOVE LIFE	17
Some Romance spreads	19
End of Chapter Activity	30
3. QUESTIONS ABOUT FAMILY MEMBERS	31
End of Chapter Activity	32
4. QUESTIONS REGARDING SPIRITUAL & LIFE PURPOSE	33
How to do a Soul Path/Purpose Reading	34
End of Chapter Activity	35
5. QUESTIONS ON CAREER/FINANCES	37
End of Chapter Activity	42
6. HOW TO GIVE A GENERAL READING	43
End of Chapter Activity	48
7. MEDIUMSHIP READING	51
Method One for a Mediumship Reading	52
Method Two for a Mediumship Reading	53
End of Chapter Activity	69
8. MY SECRET - HOW TO ANSWER A "YES/NO" QUESTION	71
Making "Yes" and "No" Answers happen for you	74
End of Chapter Activity	80

9. NEW YEAR OR BIRTHDAY READINGS 81
   End of Chapter Activity 84

10. SUICIDE, DEMON POSSESSION & READING INTERFERENCE 85
    Suicidal Clients and Loved Ones Left Behind 86
    Possessions and Attachments 86
    How to check for Interference in a Reading 88
    Great Ways to Protect Yourself During Sessions 88
    End of Chapter Activity 89

11. NAILING DOWN TIMING 91
    Predicting Timing – Simple Method 1 91
    Predicting Timing – Detailed Method 2 92
    End of Chapter Activity 96

12. HOW TO READ REVERSALS – EASY PEASY 97
    End of Chapter Activity 103

13. ASTROLOGY & NUMEROLOGY CONNECTIONS 105
    Finding Astrology Signs in Tarot 105
    Numbers and the Planets 108
    End of Chapter Activity 110

14. CARD SYMMETRY 111

15. MAJOR ARCANA AS SPIRITUAL ARCHETYPES 119
    End of Chapter Activity 120

16. ADDITIONAL KEYWORDS & SYMBOLOGY FOR THE MAJOR ARCANA 121

17. ADDITIONAL KEYWORDS & SYMBOLOGY FOR THE CUPS SUIT 145

18. ADDITIONAL KEYWORDS & SYMBOLOGY FOR THE SWORDS SUIT 159

19. ADDITIONAL KEYWORDS & SYMBOLOGY FOR THE WANDS SUIT 175

20. ADDITIONAL KEYWORDS & SYMBOLOGY FOR THE PENTACLES SUIT 189

21. RUNNING A PROFESSIONAL BUSINESS	205
Setting up your business	205
Choosing a Lucky Business Name	207
Becoming What You Promote	208
The Importance of Ethics	208
The importance of Detaching from a Client	209
The Importance of Not Being Judgey	210
Preparing the Client for a Reading - What to expect	211
End of Chapter Activity	213
22. CONCLUSION	215
Bibliography	217
About the Author	219
Also by Anmarie Uber	221

Dedicated to us. We all deserve to know our future and our options.

Tarot is the light in The Hermit's lantern, revealing the way out of darkness.

——anmarie uber

Introduction

I wrote "Fool Proof Tarot" based on my advanced tarot classes, and it includes over thirty years of insights from studying tarot, reading for clients and finding ways to help myself read better. It is written for any level of knowledge from beginner to professional and designed to help you expand your knowledge or encourage you to start doing readings professionally.

If that is not something you are interested in, this book will still benefit you and your loved ones, by covering all areas of life and helping you answer difficult questions. Whether you are reading for yourself, or someone else, the most common topics people want to know about include career, relationships, health, spiritual purpose/path, children or other family members or general readings with no particular focus. We will be looking at each of these in more depth.

If you are reading this book, you love tarot like I do, and want to learn everything you can about this fascinating prediction tool. I have found it to be a lifetime study. There is no doubt the tarot is an in-depth dive into our psyche and how we operate. It contains

INTRODUCTION

clues that uncover our strengths and weakness but also reveals the greatest mysteries to so many – our future path and what choices, if any, are available.

When it comes to actually giving a reading for yourself or someone else, doubt can creep in, even for the most experienced reader. It can be daunting to learn tarot, and whether you have just picked up a deck or have been reading for years, many find themselves still referencing a book for a card's meaning – especially when reading for yourself. Sometimes you may find yourself blanking out on a card meaning or doubting whether you are reading a card correctly etc. - myself included in this. There are surefire ways to double check yourself in this book. I wrote my first tarot book "60 Second Tarot" to help solve the above problems and this book is a continuation of that. Everyone should be reading cards with ease and confidence. Book one covers the basics of symbology and structure of the deck, allowing you to read accurately, with or without intuition. I highly recommend starting there. "Fool Proof Tarot" builds on the information from book one, giving you more confidence with clients.

Difficult questions will eventually come up, and this book is designed to help you answer them without getting stuck. In fact it will help you answer any question presented to you. Even when a client has no idea what to ask or inquire about. They just want you to "start reading", forcing you to "read in the dark" so to speak. Occasionally you get a skeptic who wants to prove you wrong – that tarot is a bunch of hoo-ha or the devil's work, so you need to be able to hold your own. Other times you just need a clear "yes" or "no". I invented this system of card reading so that you can meet these challenges and find answers every time. I hope you enjoy the tools I have laid out here. Pick what resonates and leave the rest.

Good luck on your journey to changing lives for the better and sharing your love and wisdom with those who need it.

Much Love,

Anmarie

CHAPTER 1
Answering Questions on Health

Let's be honest. It is very difficult to have a career as a psychic. People think it is all crystal balls, fairies, fun and games. But the reality is that people have real problems, and they bring those problems to you. Often because they haven't found anyone else in a so-called "normal" field who can help them. If someone's child or grandchild is terminally ill, they want the reader to tell them if there is a solution that can save the child. A reader should consider their responses very seriously. Reading on health questions can be stressful, so let's get right into how to handle this.

It is very common for a client to ask about their health or that of a loved one. When this happens, it is very important to use the words "maybe" or "I think" when describing any possible health condition you are seeing in the cards. Unless you are a licensed medical doctor or health care professional, it is outside of your scope of business to give a health diagnosis to anyone. This is why it is important to have clients sign an intake form, agreeing to your terms and conditions (see chapter on Ethics). Therefore not holding you liable or putting you in the position of being responsible for their health. Always defer to a medical professional. Statements such as, "Maybe you should make an appointment and get it checked out, just to be sure," or something similar is always a good idea.

One easy way to read on health, is to use a diagram similar to the one shown. Divide the body into nine Quadrants (more if you need them). Each quadrant represents a specific area of the body.

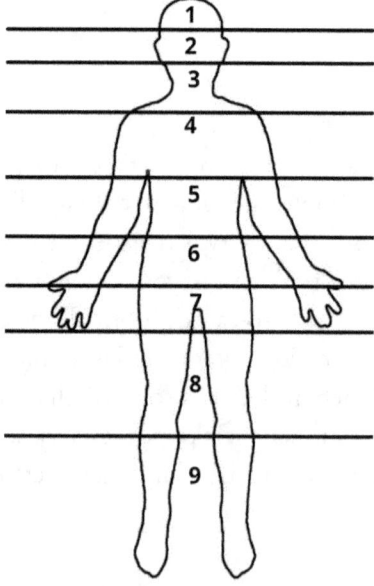

You can write into this chart what areas of the body you want to include for that Quadrant.

SOME SUGGESTIONS FOR THE QUADRANTS

- Quadrant 1 - consists of the brain, pineal, pituitary.

- Quadrant 2 - eyes, ears, nose lower brain.

- Quadrant 3 - mouth, throat, neck, thymus, thyroid.

- Quadrant 4 - shoulders, heart, lungs, breasts.

- Quadrant 5 - stomach, pancreas, kidneys, liver, gallbladder.

- Quadrant 6 - intestines, colon and low back/lumbar spine.

- Quadrant 7 - sexual reproductive organs, pelvic bone, hips.

- Quadrant 8 - thighs and knees.

- Quadrant 9 - lower legs and feet.

When doing a health spread, you will use the chart of the body and lay out cards, putting one or more in each quadrant. Here are three different ways to lay them out.

- 9 Card Spread: Lay nine cards vertically, beginning with the number one at the top of the head and ending with nine at the feet.

- 18 Card Spread: Lay out two similar rows of nine cards vertically, with one side representing the right side of the body, and the other the left.
- 27 Card Spread: For a more in-depth reading lay out three rows, one on the right, one in the center and one on the left.

This is a reference for what you will look for in each spread. There is an example of a health reading later in this chapter.

- **Reversed Cards** show which Quadrant/area of the body with a possible health issue.
- **The Suit** will tell you the cause of the issue: Wands is spiritual or etheric. It may signify energy attachments. Swords is mental. It suggests mental health or negative thought forms that can lead to emotional or physical imbalance in a particular quadrant. Cups is emotional causes or upsets that could be causing distress. Pentacles is a physical problem that has manifested in the body.
- **The Number** on the card can connect to a related Quadrant with either causal or secondary influence.
- **The Color** - There may be a color on the card that draws your eye. If so, it could represent the emotional state of the individual, which could eventually manifest as disease. It could also represent a system of the body (Depending on your interpretation of color. You can use the color lists provided in this chapter). For example red could relate to the heart or circulatory system.

Colors of Mental or Emotional States (Cups/Swords)

Thoughts and emotions are interconnected and may eventually cause disease in the body. At the very least negative thinking, depression etc. can drastically affect your quality of life. Tarot can help get to the bottom or root cause of emotional or mental upset. Colors in the cards can be signals of where the person is mentally and emotionally, and how an emotion or habitual thought process may be manifesting in the physical body. For example feeling the weight of the world on your shoulders can sometimes turn into actual shoulder pain. The suit – Swords or Cups will tell you whether this is a mental or emotional health issue.

- *Red* – Passion, desire, action, motivation, stimulation. Negative expression – Anger, abuse, hate, frustration, loss of control.

- *Orange* – Trust, openness, optimism, extroversion. Negative expression – Mistrust, resentment, closed off, isolating.

- *Yellow* – Cheerful, uplifted, sense of clarity and focus. Negative expression – Denial, feeling trapped, confusion.

- *Green* – Balanced, natural, healthy, peaceful. Negative expression – Jealous, feelings of lack, betrayal.

- *Blue* – Comforted, centered, introspective, serene. Negative expression – Depression, lonely, despondent.

- *Purple* – Intuitive, mystical, creative, imaginative. Negative expression – ungrounded, arrogant and materialistic.

- *Pink* – Hopeful, loving, compassionate. Negative expression – naïve, physical weakness, victimhood.

- *Brown* – Strong, secure, authentic. Negative expression - stagnating, helplessness, directionless.

- *Gold* – Intense, loyal, consistent. Negative expression - superficial, unreachable, lost.

- *Silver* – Imaginative, free-flowing, adaptive. Negative expression – moody, cold, mean-spirited.

- *White* – Free, complete, light-hearted. Negative expression – noncommittal, sorrowful, doomed.

- *Black* – Safe, reclusive, introverted. Negative expression - trapped, stifled, empty.

Colors to Represent Organs/Systems of the Body (Pentacles)

- *White* - skeletal – bones, joints, teeth, skull, cartilage

- *Yellow* - digestive – mouth, small intestine, pancreas, liver, stomach, salivary

- *Purple* - endocrine – glands that secrete hormones and regulate the entire body

- *Orange* - muscular – muscles, fascia, tendons, ligaments

- *Brown/tan/dark yellow* - excretory – skin, bladder, kidneys, liver, lungs, large intestine

- *Green* - reproductive – ovaries, testes, uterus, sexual organs

- *Pink* - nervous – nerves, spinal cord, brain

- *Blue* - respiratory – lungs, air passages, nose, mouth, pharynx, trachea, bronchial tubes

- *Red* – circulatory/cardiovascular – blood, lymph, heart, vascular – veins, arteries, capillaries

- *Black* - removal due to surgery or tumor

- *Gray* - possible problem developing

- *Gold/Silver* - vibrant health

LAYING OUT THE HEALTH SPREAD EXERCISE

1. Decide beforehand which Quadrant will refer to what organ or system of the body or use my suggestions. Make this the same every time so you do not wonder what a card means. Also decide what colors relate to each of those systems or organs for you. Example: White represents teeth, or Quadrant 3 represents the mouth.
2. Lay out the cards in your choice of the 9, 18 or 27 spread configurations following the 9 Quadrants of the body chart. The 9 Card Spread is a quick overview of a client's health, using 1 card for each Quadrant. The 18 or 27 Card Spread gives a more detailed look,

using two cards for each Quadrant to signify right and left side of the body, or three cards in each Quadrant adding a middle card for the center or back of the body.
3. Next, begin to look for reversals which show a problem area. Which quadrant is the reversed card in? Is it on the right or left side of the body? Both? What system or organs relate to that quadrant? For example, a reversed card in quadrant 3 tells you there is a problem with the body in that area. This could represent the throat or thyroid or whatever you assigned to that quadrant.
4. What is the suit of the card? The suit will tell you what is causing the issue. Pentacles is for a definite issue in the physical body that has manifested. Swords and Cups signify mental or emotional attitudes/patterns that could lead to a problem. Wands could relate to the aura or attachments.
5. Are there any colors that stand out in a reversed card which may define more detail? Colors can signify a more specific issue, such as Quadrant 3 and the color white. Quadrant 3 is mouth, white is teeth. Which side the reversed card is on is where in the mouth – right or left side. Front or back?
6. Or maybe a color is significant in several cards (this may represent a systemic or whole-body issue or overall thought pattern if the suit is cups or swords signifying a mental/emotional problem).
7. What is the number on the reversed card? It can point to other quadrants that could be connected to or causing the issue.

'FOOL' PROOF TAROT

An Example of the 9 Card Spread:

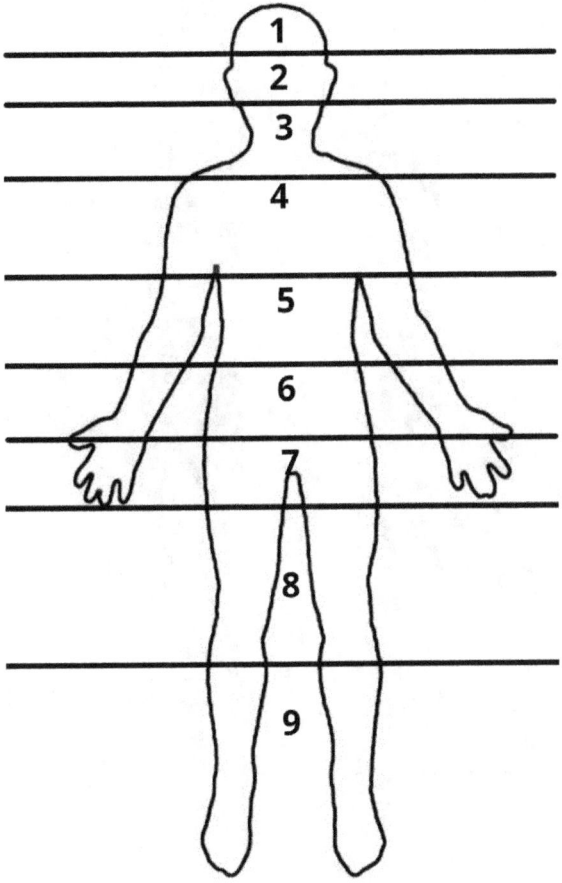

ANMARIE UBER

In this 9 Spread you see four reversed cards. Card 1 - Quadrant 1 is suggesting something with the brain. Card 2 is the eyes, ears, nose. Card 6 is suggesting something digestive or intestinal. Card 7 is eliminative, sexual organs or hips. The next step you would look for are clues using color for additional information. Looking at numbers, you will notice Card 6 is a 3. Card 6 issues could be related to the third Quadrant. Card 7 is a 1 and could be related to the first Quadrant. This person has problems with signals in the brain, swelling in the nasal tissue, ongoing digestive problems and constipation. And low back issues (card 6 area)

which are causing sciatica down going through the hips. The digestive issues could be related to the endocrine system represented by the pituitary/pineal/adrenal and thyroid. They can be caused by the suits. Card 1 being an actual physical problem (pentacles). Card 2 being an upset in the auric field (wands). Card 6 is also wands. Card 7 is the Sun which can represent all of the above.

The 18 Card Health reading:

This is done similar to the 9 Card reading but will give more detail. For the 18 Card Spread, you will envision a line going down the center of the body. The right card will be the right side of the body, front and back. The left card will represent the left side of the body, front and back. Knowing which side of the body helps narrow in where the problems lie. Follow the tips for using reversals, colors, suits and numbers.

An Example of the 27 Card Spread:

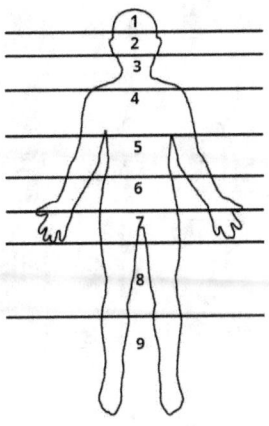

ANMARIE UBER

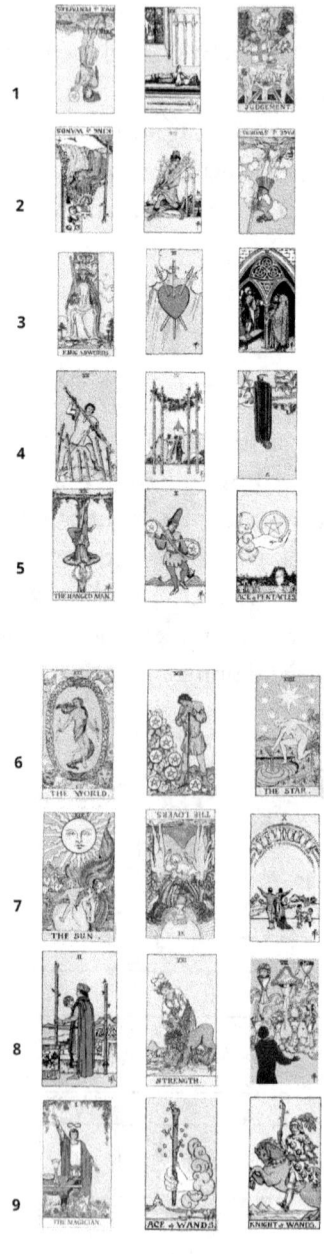

(Note: you will have to decide ahead of time which side of the picture represents right and left. How you are looking at the person which would be your right/left, or the person's actual right/left side. The middle cards represent middle of the body or the back side.)

1. Right side of Quadrant 1 there is a physical problem on the right side. This person has migraines that affect the right side of the head. The color orange is jumping out at me on the Page of Pentacles, which would suggest muscular tension. Pentacles – some kind of actual physical problem in the brain waves or functioning. There is no number on the card which says the issues are contained in the head.
2. The second Quadrant is interesting, as it shows a reversed card on both sides of the body. This represents eyes, ears and nose. The color red is popping, which is circulations, veins, etc. The subject experiences a trigger in the migraines through loud noises, breathing in chemical perfumes and the eyes go off balance. Swords is mental stress, wands represent outside entity aura field interference (triggers of perfumes that cause the migraines, etc. Also, possible dark entity interference). There are no numbers on the cards, so the issue remains in that area.
3. The next reversed card is the Five of Cups in Quadrant 4. This person also has an old injury in the left shoulder. Emotional beliefs may be tied into this injury and why it won't heal. Feelings of overwhelm is causing the individual not to take time to stretch and heal the injury, causing flare-ups of pain. It is a 5 and related to Quadrant 5. The individual has poor

posture and the curve of the spine may be causing the old injury of the shoulder to act up.
4. Quadrant 6 with 7 of Pentacles reversed in the center position says something in the mid body area of that Quadrant. But because this person has low back pain that radiates into the hips, it made me pay attention to the number 7, which means the problem in Quadrant 6 is related to Quadrant 7. Quadrant has a reversed card in the center as well – the Lovers 6 – which solidifies these two are connected, as this number in position 7 relates back to Quadrant 6. So, the problem (pentacles) is in quadrant 6. The orange color in the 7 of Pentacles is jumping out at me which relates to muscles, fascia, tendons and ligaments. This is good news, meaning the pain in the low back is muscular, not bone, and can be massaged, stretched and helped to heal.

Here is a video with variations on the 27 Card Spread.
www.youtube.com/watch?v=UOmusG4grx8&t=552s

Major Arcana Health Spread

A quick way to read on a person's health would be to assign a bodily system and/or major organ to each Major Arcana card. So, when these cards are dealt out you know what area it is relating to. For example, the High Priestess has pomegranates on the veil behind her. These represent the female ovaries. The palms represent the male organs. This card could mean problems in these areas if you decide to assign this card to the reproductive systems.

How to do the Major Arcana Spread:

Simply shuffle the cards and begin to deal straight from the top of the deck. Lay out cards until a Major Arcana card comes up. Leave that card out and shuffle again. Ask if there are any more issues in the body. Pull the first card off the top. If it is a

Major Arcana, then this is a second issue. If it is not, you will focus on the Major Arcana card you initially drew. Notice any colors, numbers, suits or other information you are drawn to, and utilize the charts already given to interpret the card with mine or your own meanings.

END OF CHAPTER ACTIVITY

1. Map out your Quadrants, and what areas of the body will apply to each.
2. Assign colors or use my suggestions to correspond to different systems/organs of the body.
3. Practice giving a health reading on yourself or someone else, using the 9, 18 and 27 card spreads.

CHAPTER 2
Questions on Love Life

Ahhh...romance. It is all roses and chocolates, and whispering sweet nothings...or is it? The truth is there are dangerous psychopaths stalking people, abused husbands/wives, people terrified to leave a relationship because they will be financially destitute...and yes, there are those readings where it is the giddy happy soulmate romance of a lifetime. Are you ready for all of it? How to answer questions on the love life. Who is my soulmate? Do I have a Twin Flame? Is the girl I'm dating now my Twin?

It is fun to ponder if a knight in shining armor is coming to your aid or a princess of your happily ever after needs rescuing, but relationships are not always fairytales and can be difficult to navigate. They come in all shapes and sizes. From gay couples or straight, happy-in-love couples and married spouses, to mistresses, death and divorce, relationships can cause a great deal of stress. Relationship questions may even involve someone widowed and looking to enter the dating arena again. Even though relationship readings may seem frivolous or fun on the surface, they can be messy and could possibly deal with serious consequences. Not to mention any children involved. So, like every other section in this book, realize that this is real life and you have to consider what you say.

It is not a time to be judgmental or bring your personal or religious beliefs into the discussion. Remember, this is their life. You are going to try to guide their soul to make the best decisions possible for their future. Sometimes this doesn't always follow a logical opinion but may require some logical counseling on your part. For example: A woman comes in and asks if she should stay with her husband. She is getting physically beat up by him. You have to weigh your reading very carefully. Logically, your initial reaction is to tell her to get out of there. But maybe if she takes your advice, he ends up following her and tries to kill her. This is not uncommon in these situations. Or she may not be ready, and will just go back to him, as she identifies abuse as love. It can be a tricky tight-rope walk.

When in doubt, always send them to a professional counselor if that is possible. In this situation, I would look to people around the person. Will they have support/protection, if they leave? Did their soul choose this experience. What is their emotional/mental state? What can they handle? Are children involved?

Obviously not all relationship questions are going to be this drastic, but again I cannot stress this enough (after having countless bad readings and advice) - try to remember that this is real life, and you are a neutral party doing your best to give guidance.

SOME ROMANCE SPREADS

Tarot Spread for a New Partner

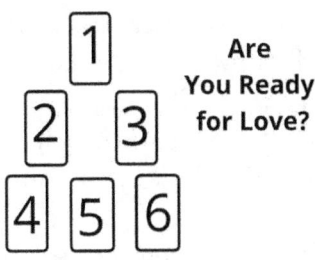

Maybe someone has just had a partner pass away. Or went through a divorce. Or have been hurt very badly and have little to no self-love. Maybe they are running patterns attracting the same type of partner over and over. It might be time to first see if they are ready for a relationship.

1. Are you ready? When love comes, will you be ready to welcome it? Do you have the door open? (If no, you may want to try the spread "Healing your blocks to love".

Card 1 - Any blocks to your readiness will appear in the first card. Such as your own fears, other people, past lovers etc. This card should be studied. If the following cards show a pattern of a dysfunctional lover coming in...then it means your energy field needs clearing, cords cut and you need to let go of any previous relationships, as you could be pulling in the same type again. Card 1 needs to be addressed.

2. Potential Lover - What are they like? Personality, physical features, financial situation, emotional state.

Card 2 - Pay attention to the suit if there is one, for information either positive or negative about specific areas of the person's life. Draw three more cards for more clarity about this person, so you get a more detailed image. If you get a Court card, what are the physical appearance attributes of that suit? If you get a Pentacles card, and it is the 5, does this person have money issues? Etc.

3. How you meet - Where or how do you meet?

Card 3 - Is there a person that introduces you? Do you meet online? Certain cards such as Queens and Kings represent people. Other cards such as the Tower or 8 of wands could suggest online, etc.

4. Will this relationship bring you happiness long term?

5. Will this relationship bring your partner happiness long term?

For Card 4 and 5 - positive looking cards here will give you a yes or no answer. If no, ask if there is a another partner coming in who is a better fit for you, and draw another card for a yes or no. If "no" again, you may want to go back to card 1 and draw a few more cards for clarity, to gain insight how you or your circumstances are blocking someone from coming in (you are afraid, you don't trust, you haven't removed the energy from a previous lover, etc.)

6. The number or suit on this card suggests a timing for when you will meet this person.

Card 6 - Pay attention to what you are drawn to in the card for the timing. (See Chapter 11 on timing.)

Example of a reading:

Card 1 – Are you ready? When love comes, will you be ready to welcome it? Do you have the door open?

Knight of Wands – The moving card – ready to move forward.

Card 2 – Potential Lover - What are they like? Personality, physical features, financial situation, emotional state.

3 of Cups reversed – An emotional person(cups). A good

communicator (3). Someone who is upbeat or celebrates life. Someone commitment minded. Future-oriented. Lighter hair, hazel eyes (cups). If you read reversals, this could be someone who sucks the joy out of people, unbalanced emotionally.

Card 3 - How you meet - Where or how do you meet?

Wheel of Fortune reversed – You have known them before. It represents karma. They pop up unexpectedly. With a reversal here, this may not be good luck.

Card 4 - Will this relationship bring you happiness long term?

Death Reversed – It will create endings so that a new life can begin. It will be different from the old. With a reversal here, the positive qualities of Death, such as changes that you wanted could be changes that are not good for you. This could be a no. Since I take the Death card as a no, I asked if there was someone better than this one coming. I picked another card and drew the Sun card, which means happiness and a "yes". So, there may be a person coming first in that sucks joy represented by the Death card, followed by a person represented by the Sun card. It's important to pay attention to the red flags and be able to say "no" (I talk more about red flags near the end of this chapter).

Card 5 - Will this relationship bring your partner happiness long term?

2 of Cups – A karmic relationship. This partner sees you as their soulmate. They may be getting more from you, than you from them.

Card 6 - The number or suit on this card suggests a timing for when you will meet this person.

Queen of Cups – This is my card, so if this was my reading, I am the decision-maker on not only the timing, but how this plays out. It looks like I need to say "no" to this first person at the first red flag. Using my intuition (cups) will tell me all I need to know. Don't listen to my head. If it feels wrong, it is wrong.

Tarot Spread: Healing Your Blocks to Love

1. What you are searching for? Does this card reveal something that you really want, or does it show an old pattern? Is it a positive or negative image?

2. Blocks currently holding you back, if any. Or blessings helping you. Is this card positive or negative?

3. Emotional or mental readiness.

4. Is your soul ready? Is a partner on your path at this current time?

5. What type of partner would you make for the other person? This card reveals what they get from you. What kind of partner are you? What are you bringing to the table? Does this card reveal something that needs to be addressed in yourself first? Or does this card show you are ready? If not, take some time for self-heal-

ing, releasing the past, forgiveness, or getting your life in shape - such as financially, emotionally or otherwise.

Tarot Spread for Someone You Have Already Met

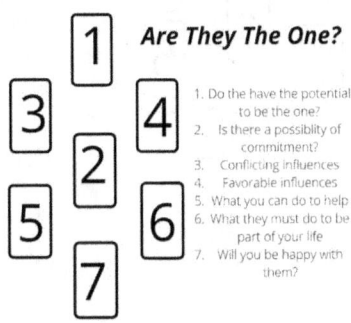

Are They The One?
1. Do the have the potential to be the one?
2. Is there a possiblity of commitment?
3. Conflicting influences
4. Favorable influences
5. What you can do to help
6. What they must do to be part of your life
7. Will you be happy with them?

Example:

Card 1 – Empress – "Yes". (See Chapter 8 on yes or no answers).

Card 2 – Queen of Wands, a card representing a person. Someone is standing in the way, or it is up to one of the parties involved to decide or be open to commitment – you, the partner or someone else.

Card 3 – Page of Swords. A child has to be considered.

Card 4 – 3 of Wands. Opportunities coming to help.

Card 5 – 8 of Cups. Let go of emotional dissatisfaction or the past. Move forward.

Card 6 – Knight of wands. Moving card. Possibly this is a long-distance relationship.

Card 7 – 10 of Cups. "Yes." Future happiness.

A Tarot Spread for Current Relationship/Marriage

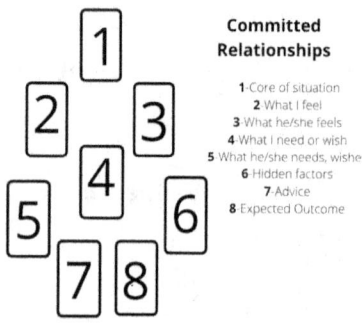

Red Flags in a Partner - Character Flaws Vs. Issues

When assessing a possible future mate -or one you are already involved with, live with or are committed to – you will first need to differentiate between deal-breakers and issues. A deal-breaker is a character flaw. An issue is a personality trait that may require understanding and love, but instead annoys the partner because it is different from their own personality.

An issue can look something like this...Sarah is insecure about her appearance. She constantly seeks compliments which annoys her husband Bill - who is confident about his own looks, sees Sarah as pretty and doesn't understand her insecurity. Next, Sarah begins to talk down about herself because she is not getting the reassurance she needs back from Bill. Now the couple thinks they have a problem, but it is not a problem at all. It can be as simple as understanding where this insecurity originated and helping Sarah to heal or give support. Sarah having the issue of insecurity about her looks is not going to cause harm or damage to Bill. Rather it is just irritating or a turn off for him. It is actually a call for love. A call for help and support from Bill, not an irritation. Sarah is not doing this to deliberately be annoying.

An issue is something the couple can heal together – if both parties are willing. Some areas may be too sensitive to talk about. But reaching a compromise on how you communicate love and support to one another can be done. This builds trust, and maybe someday Sarah will open up about her insecurity with Bill. There are many books, videos, podcasts, counselors and any number of resources to help you navigate a relationship. A good suggestion is the book, "The 5 Love Languages". If the partner is *unwilling* to read this book or make an effort to do so (it comes in audio too, so no excuses) you may have someone with character flaws, or someone who doesn't care enough about you or the relationship to make such a simple effort as listening to a book. Find out what the issue is. Is it their own insecurity of feeling threatened by what the book may reveal about themselves, or is it laziness in making an effort?

Another example of an issue: One partner is bad with handling money. They can't keep track of how much they have, or when the bills are due. Some people's minds work in different ways, such as creative, mechanical, numerical, organized or structured. A creative type may find it difficult to follow a regimented schedule, as their mind can easily wander and lose track of time. Then they stress and end up being late. Numbers and details may escape them, but broad concepts make complete sense to them. They end up having money and spending issues because they cannot seem to discipline their mind to keep track of the details. Another person sees the world in all the minute details. They find it easy to focus their mind on structured and repetitive tasks. It is easy for them to manage schedules and bank balances. This partner would be ideal for taking over the finances in the relationship, as that is one of their strengths. If both partners have trouble managing finances, they may need to hire trustworthy outside to help take care of the problem.

In this scenario, the structured partner takes the reins and controls the money. They get the bills paid and the creative partner gets spending allowance for the month. The creative partner now needs to pick up slack in another area – such as taking on more cleaning or cooking duties around the house to make up for the extra load the methodical partner will now have to do. These are agreements that can be settled between grown-ups. Always Remember: If you didn't get into the relationship to *give* love... meaning you are only there to get something...then the relationship will never succeed. It means you are a taker. However, you also have to have balance. You need two givers. If you have a giver and a taker, the giver suffers.

Should I Stay or Go?

Red flags signal takers caused by flaws in the character that lead to bad choices. Meaning something is inherently off with this person, making them incapable of having a relationship at this time – or possibly ever. Issues as explained previously can be worked on together. Character flaws are an innate problem because they cause harm to the partner involved with this person. Some character flaws can be solved...*But the person with the problems has to be the one to do it - before getting into a relationship. And they need to show a track record that the problem has been solved over a long period of time, before they should be considering entering into any intimate relationship.*

Character flaws destroy your emotional, mental, financial, social, family and physical health.

Examples of Character Flaws:

- *Drug addiction* – Meaning the person is unable/unwilling to stop using a substance. Escapism. They are not present emotionally, physically or mentally to join in a healthy relationship. If this drug is helping to treat a health condition, this is different, and not in the category of willing drug abuse. In a drug abuse relationship, you the other partner will only suffer. Your family or children will suffer. Your finances will suffer. The addict will at some point stop contributing in that area, if they ever were. They may be unable to work, constantly get fired or just don't want to work. They don't card. The cost of drugs will drain finances dry, and you may find yourself dealing with drug lords, legal issues, imprisonment, fines etc. How could this relationship EVER help you? Living with a drug addict means you are left with only two choices: tolerate it or leave. There is no in-between. No hard love. No helping. They have to be the ones to do it. You have to be the one to leave. Otherwise, your life will continue to be dragged down with them. Or you might possibly join them in the drug abuse. Not to mention the dark entities and portals opened by living or relating with this person (see Chapter on possessions, attachments – this is a real thing). Drug abuse includes alcohol, illegal drugs, prescription drugs, recreational etc.

Realize this does not apply to someone who has chosen to end the abuse and has a record behind them to show they are serious. And they are continuing to work on themselves emotionally, mentally, physically and spiritually (removing attachments that keep talking in their ear, telling them to go back to the drugs, causing depression, low self-esteem etc. and all-around draining them dry of soul energy – just because the drugs are gone, the entity can remain behind). Otherwise, the addiction is gone, but the addictive personality remains, and you still suffer. Kudos to those who have chosen to help themselves and found the strength to say, "No. I am more valuable than this. I am not this drug. I am not an addict. I am not a person who abuses drugs." This individual has chosen hope and made a change to a new life.

What to do if you are intimately involved with a drug addict: Get professional advice. Get out of the situation as soon as you are able. Find outside help if needed. Do not be in a house where illegal activities are taking place as you will be liable as well if they are caught. Or in danger if a drug lord knocks on your door looking to be paid. Ask yourself, "Is this an environment for a sovereign being? For my children?" Etc. If the answer is, "No," then find a way out.

- *A narcissist, sociopath, borderline personality disorder or other diagnosed mental disorder that will make your life a living nightmare.* These people play mental games with you, that can turn physical or dangerous. They can isolate you, make everything about themselves which makes you feel like you don't exist and a number of other abusive techniques. You will want to do some research into this to see if you could possibly be with one of these people – and get a professional diagnosis for them if possible - but chances are, you already know.

- *Having a violent nature, stalking and predatorial behaviors (psychopaths).* You absolutely must get law enforcement and other professionals involved. There needs to be records of what incidents have transpired.

- *A careless gambler or someone who takes huge deliberate risks with your financial well-being.* They quit jobs on a whim. Refuse to pay bills or child support to an ex because they think they shouldn't have to. This is not talking about someone who may be bad at managing money, but are working hard to earn their share. It also does not mean someone who is in debt but working hard to pay it off. This is someone who will deliberately take you into bankruptcy, or make you work yourself to death supporting them, without a care for how it affects you. If they are physically capable of working, they should be. If not, they should seek assistance (i.e. disability etc.). If they don't work a job, then they should be contributing in other ways to maintain the household. Regardless, they cannot be a funnel or sieve under your financial income and security. You cannot be in a relationship with this person. You will have little to no options for your future, will work yourself to the grave trying to get out of the financial hole, and spend your life always trying to catch up. If you are already in this situation, leave as soon as humanly possible. Life is short. On the other hand, if you are independently wealthy, then this is your decision, although this type of financial gambler tends to have some of the other character flaws.

- *A taker living off the sweat of your back.* This person can fall into one or more of the previous categories. Maybe they have an addiction, and you have to support them. Maybe they are a narcissist and don't believe they have to do their part. Maybe they are violent and use threats to continue their "taker" behavior. You know if you are living with one of these types – because you do all the giving. And probably keep hoping at some point they will give back. But they are not like you. And you have to consider getting out.

END OF CHAPTER ACTIVITY

1. Read on your own love life, choosing one or more of the spreads in this chapter. If you are single, read for someone else close to you that can give feedback.
2. Analyze your own relationships for issues or character flaws. The more experience you have with relationships, the more you can advise others.

CHAPTER 3
Questions About Family Members

Often clients will ask for information about other people. It is usually about family members such as children, spouse, parents etc. But what if those individuals don't want your client...or you for that matter...to know their particulars? This is understandably a common situation. Let's talk about what to do when a client asks you to read about another person.

First you will need to explain that you may not get all the information they are seeking, because the individuals they are asking about may want privacy on certain matters. Then refocus the reading on the client's relationship with this person, instead of revealing personal details about what the other person is doing or will do. For example, your client wants to know more about a guy their adult daughter is dating. You can take a look at him, but know that not everything is going to come up or should come up about this person. Instead ask things like, "Can he make the daughter happy?" "What is their role as parent in this, if anything?" Overall this is a private affair between the daughter and the boyfriend, no matter how much the parent worries or wants to help.

If you see something dangerous – such as possible harm coming to the daughter, it may be important to mention that this could be a possibility and the parent should keep an eye on the situation. Referrals to professional help are always the best option.

END OF CHAPTER ACTIVITY

1. If you anticipate doing readings as a professional (or already are), prepare a script of what you will tell clients who want detailed information about other peoples' lives. It should be polite but help them understand that this is not always possible (or in some cases, ethical).
2. Spend some time releasing your fears surrounding your own family, their expectations of you, your expectations of them, and anything else that can free you to walk your path while allowing others to walk theirs.

CHAPTER 4

Questions Regarding Spiritual & Life Purpose

The most common questions I get in relation to a person's spiritual life is, "Am I on my path?" and "What am I here to do?" A lot of people feel as if they are failing at life. They have somehow gone off course or do not understand what their soul purpose is. Many times, the answer is found in their past lives on Earth or prior to those incarnations. Where is their origin point? Where did they come from and how is that affecting their present life? Ultimately you can't tell another person the specifics of their spiritual path – as they have to uncover this for themselves - but you can give them a general overview and insight of who they are as a soul.

The Astro Wheel Spread which follows is a great tool to use for the spiritual path of the soul. You can look at card 1 to see what the individual is here to do in this present life. Card 12 to see where they have been in previous lifetimes before this one, and how all the cards tie together. The intentions or experiences in those past lives create material the individual wants to resolve, avoid or finish up in this present life. Did they come from somewhere beyond Earth? The answer can be found in these two cards, or in a center card. Did the Star card pop up? Or cards that suggest other dimensions?

Many times, the Fool and World together can suggest a final lifetime incarnation. The 3 cards in the center of the circle will reveal the overarching theme of their life. The other positions show areas of life where their purpose is playing out. Also look for wands cards to give hints of their spiritual path, and any cards numbered 7 for spiritual life.

HOW TO DO A SOUL PATH/PURPOSE READING

Astro Spread

Lay out the Astro Wheel and study card 12 (the inner self and where you were prior to this lifetime) and card 1 (current self in the world and what your soul is here to do in this lifetime). Use the numbers and suits in the cards to help with interpretation. The symbology in the picture may also link your mind to past life information. Next, connect the other cards to these two, tying in more information to help with the interpretation of card 1 and 12, filling in details of your past lives and current purpose. The whole circle of cards can be connected to 1 and 12, as well as the 3 cards in the middle relating to the 3 past lives that correlate or overlap with your current one. Major Arcana can hint to what stage of spiritual awakening you are in but these twenty-two cards, although in forward numbered progression don't necessarily follow any one linear direction. You can be at any stage or jump to the end when it is time. For the card positions, see Chapter 6 on General readings.

END OF CHAPTER ACTIVITY

Do some further exploring into your past lives, Akashic Records or other active meditations, to discover your roots and why your soul came here at this time.

CHAPTER 5

Questions on Career/Finances

In today's world, money makes the world go round. It can ease your mind and be a blessing, or it can break up a relationship, cause a person to give up on life and determine whether your children have food on the table. Acquiring money usually involves stress in the workplace and can lead to health issues. Let's discuss how to tackle the touchy subject of career and finance in a reading.

The most important thing a reader can do is give a person hope. Especially when it comes to finances and career. To some it is their very identity, and without it they believe they are directionless, having little to no worth. For most people, a career (as opposed to a job) is akin to a dream. Their dream of a life for themselves. Work that is satisfying and brings a sense of expression, contribution and accomplishment. Money represents freedom and the ability to have control over one's life. A career can be anything from a housewife/husband to owning a multi-million-dollar corporation. It is a way of fulfilling their place in the world, by using their talents, interests and knowledge to express themselves.

The money earned gives them a means of support to continue their dream.

A lot of people give up on their dreams and take on a job because their immediate survival requires it. And then there are some that believe money is everything and will do anything to get it. Either way, you as a reader are here to help them. The thing holding them back from a fulfilling life is usually a decision or a determination to have what they want. And that leaves you with the job of identifying the obstacles and available options. What career is a fit for them? If it isn't showing in the cards, what needs to be done to find it? What attitudes need to change. There is always an avenue for money to flow into someone's life.

A new career can be started at any stage of life. Or can be done to some degree. For example, let's say a person always wanted to be a doctor and never went to med school. Instead of a doctor they became a teacher. Now they are sixty years old and do not want to invest the time required to become a doctor or take on that school debt. Maybe instead, they could take a few classes on nutrition and use their teaching skills to teach others online about nutrition? There is always a way to fulfill a dream.

A great spread to use for career and finance is the Astro Spread from the previous chapter. Cards 1, 2, 5, 6, 7, 8 and 10 can give great insight. Card 1 is their life path. Card 2 represents money, values and income. Card 5 represents hobbies that bring enjoyment or possible business ideas. Card 6 shows everyday work. Card 7 represents possible business partners. Card 8 is other people's money, investors, or money coming in or going out due to legal issues. Card 10 is the career or job. In addition, card 11 is the network they have around them, including co-workers. Card

4 is their home life, and how that is supporting or challenging their career. The center cards may relate to another card by sharing the same number or sitting near the card. Also, any Major Arcana cards in a spread can give clues to what type of profession suits you or whether you would be a better fit for self-employment. The Court Card representing their significator (their astrology sign – see Chapter 13) can also give clues to a possible profession. The suit of Pentacles represents actual money coming in, and the Suit of Wands represents business.

For a quick answer to finding a suitable career, separate the Major Arcana from the deck and draw one or more cards to represent possible careers for the individual. Then match them to the career choices listed at the end of this chapter. If the card doesn't feel accurate for them, look at the number on the card and refer to the other corresponding cards with that same number. Such as if the 1 Magician careers do not feel right for the person, look to the 10 Wheel of Fortune and 19 The Sun. Option two is to keep the deck together and deal off the top of the deck until a Major Arcana cards come up. Drawing a clarifying Minor Arcana card after that can fill in more details.

Possible Career Choices

0 Fool
 Comedian, Rock Climber, Unemployed, Philosopher

1 Magician
 Sales, Entertainment, Retail, Hair Stylist, Public Speaker, Inventor

. . .

2 High Priestess –
Librarian, Historian, Psychologist, Psychic, Detective

3 Empress
Fashion Designer, Artist, Beauty Industry, Home Décor, Housewife, Mid-wife, Landscaper, Park Ranger

4 Emperor
Government, Military, Self-Employed, Corporate CEO, Manager, Real Estate Investor, Politician

5 Heirophant
Church official, School Teacher, Counselor, Coach, Advisor, Salesperson

6 Lovers
Advertising, Communication Field, Business Partnership, Marriage Counselor

7 Chariot
Car Sales, Driver, Pilot, Realtor, Astrologer, Flight Attendant, Mechanic

8 Strength
Zoologist, Dentist, Body Builder, Veterinarian, Animal Communicator, Nurse

9 Hermit
Monk, Writer, Author, Software Developer, Work from home, Off-grid Living, Scientist

10 Wheel
Investor, Casinos, Editing, Proofreaders, Prognosticator, Statistician

11 Justice
Attorney, Judge, Paralegal, Auditor, Rights Activist, Child Protection Services

12 Hanged Man -
Yoga Instructor, Visionary, Chiropractor, Poet, Gymnast, Remote Viewer, Programmer

13 Death
Funeral business, Tax Collector, Insurance, Life Coach, Stockbroker, Medium, Banker

14 Temperance
Chemist, Mediator, Investor, Pharmacist, Bartender, Cook, Economist, Liquids

15 Devil
Substance Abuse or Sex Counselor, Restaurant, Food Industry, Tobacco or Alcohol Industry, Manual Labor

. . .

16 Tower
   Computers, Construction, Engineer, Electrician, Architect, Firefighter

17 Star
   Celebrity, Massage Therapist, Spa Owner or Technician, Healer, Financial Advisor, Astronomer, Physician

18 Moon
   Psychic, Gynecologist, Sailor, Oceanography, Psychiatrist, Plumber, Jail or Prison System

19 Sun
   Childcare, Education, Equestrian, CEO, Distributor, Agriculture

20 Judgement
   Cell phones, Wireless Technology, Musician, Inventor, Technology Advancement

21 World
   Travel, Online Business, Social Justice, Environment, World Leader

END OF CHAPTER ACTIVITY

Draw a Major Arcana card and see if it relates to you and your talents and interests.

CHAPTER 6
How to give a General Reading

When a client does not have a specific area of concern or come in with questions, it can seem challenging to read for them - especially when you are just starting out. More often than not, this is the case. Many come to readings unprepared or not knowing what to expect. It is up to you then, to guide the session. Let's get into how to read with little to no direction or information.

Using the Astro Wheel is very helpful for general readings, as it covers many areas of a person's life and gives a snapshot overview. Reading the Astro spread will help spark questions and bring up topics the client may want to delve into further. A study of the twelve astrology houses that relate to this spread will enrich and enhance your interpretations.

The three cards in the center show a theme in the person's life at the moment. With this life blueprint, you get a quick overview of what is going on in all areas of the person's life and can add a card or two for clarity if needed.

ANMARIE UBER

Astro Spread

This spread can also predict what is coming for them in the future month/year. If the current month was April, card 1 would represent April Card 2 would be May. If you want to do the next twelve days, card 1 would be today; card 2 tomorrow; card 3 is day three, etc.

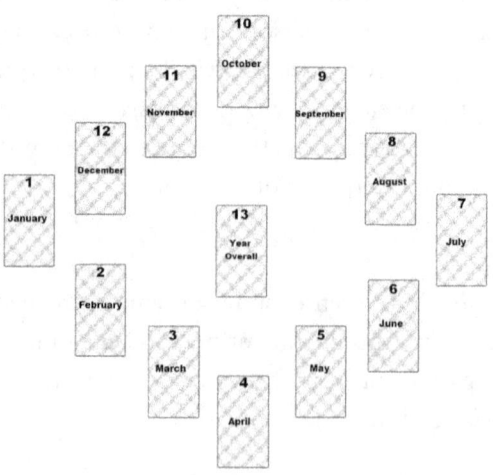

Here are the position meanings, taken from book one in my tarot series:

1st – Represents you, your outer personality, aspects of your character and how others see you. Also: Ego, body type, childhood experience, leadership qualities, personality, view of the world, 1st impression you make on others, defense mechanisms, face, body, self.

2nd – Money, what you value. Also: The outer resources available to the individual, material things, safety, security, possessions, attitude toward food with 6th house, self-worth, noble or base values.

3rd – Short trips, your mind, Siblings. Also: Mental gifts, learning and teaching, school up to college, outside world, cars buses, trains, ability to learn, the way your mind works, positive/negative thinking, communication - writing, reading, talking, teaching, letters, magazines, newspapers, near relatives, neighbors, neighborhood, radio, TVs, i-pads, phones, computers.

4th – Your home, house and what's going on there. Also: Your sanctuary, roots, conditions in old age, attitude toward family, ability to nurture people emotionally, real estate, land, gardening, your father, your mother, country of birth, mines, graves, underground places, quirks or abilities passed on to you from parents, especially from father, genetics.

5th – Love affairs, Children, Thing you do to have fun or love to do such as hobbies. Also: Fatherhood, drama, theater, art, ability to be creative, taking risks, gambling, investing, schools, resorts, games and sports, ability to give and receive love, perception of the love you got as a child, childlike/childish qualities, ability to be romantic.

6th – Everyday work, small pets, health. Also: diets, food, attitude toward cleanliness and order, old relatives, obligations, your employees, ability to be inventive, taste in clothes, servants, uncles and aunts on father's side, community needs, weather as it affects your health.

7th – Partner, marriage, business partner(s). Also: clients, best friends and peers, mentors, live-in relationships, known enemies, dealings with the public, contracts, art, diplomacy, social urges, grandparents.

8th – Other People's money, legal issues, soulmates, taxes. Also: Endings and beginnings, love interaction from the other from the 7th house, deep Merging Box, secrets, psychology, therapy, psychiatry, astrology, yoga, detective work, psychic abilities, sex, great change brought about by crisis, death, legacies and wills, hidden talents, ability to be reborn and ability to be alone.

9th – Long distance travel, college/university, your spiritual philosophy. Also: Rewards, higher understanding, higher education, mind expansion, gurus, religions, foreign countries, import/export business, publishing, hard cover books, mass circulation magazines, international anything, travel, large enterprises, in-laws, lawyers, judges, lawsuits, the law, faith.

. . .

10 – Your reputation, Career. Also: Your role in life, public Image, the parent who was the main authority, credit or lack thereof, people with power over you, bosses, government, attitude toward authority figures, sense of duty, power, public eye, homosexuality, promotions.

11 – Your support network of friends, social circles. Also: Enemies, Idealism, past-life enemies who are now friends, associates, income from main profession, the parent who dominated you, peer groups, advice you get for good or ill, advisors, your hopes, wildest dreams, clubs, other people's children.

12 – Your hidden inner self, that you may or may not be aware of, the inner self that others probably don't see. How we are all one and connected. Also: The characteristics, of your most recent past life, behind the scenes, God, prison, bondage, confinement, hospitals, large institutions, hidden enemies, everyday saints, psychiatry/psychology – how you mess yourself up, large animals, mother's relatives, escapist tendencies, unconscious, psychic abilities, healing abilities, selflessness, karma and past lives, to serve or suffer, victim, the past.

Card 13, 14 and 15 - Represent major themes going on right now, and usually apply to more than one area of life. One of these cards next to, above or below another card, is related to that card. You can also look at their number and apply it to a house(s) to see its connection to that area. For example: The Sun card in the center is a great card to have as an overlying influence on the spread. Its number is 19, which is 10 and 1, (when added together), so it can apply to cards 10 and 1. etc. Overall, the Sun is influencing all the houses because it is in the center.

. . .

Another great spread to use for general readings is the Celtic Cross. Card 1, 2 and 3 will give insight into the main issue going on with the person right now. This will give a focus to the reading and the suits can be used for clarification. Wands is spiritual/creative/business matters, cups is emotional or romantic, swords is mental or worries/obstacles and pentacles is physical/financial. If there are a lot of one suit in the spread, that is also an indicator of the subject matter, or what is the current theme in this person's life.

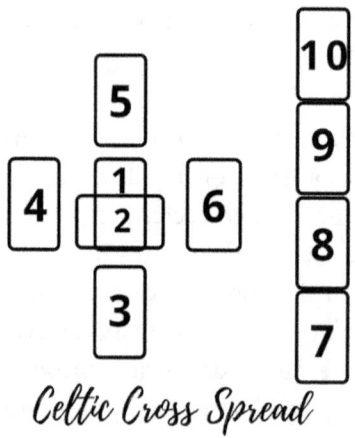

Celtic Cross Spread

END OF CHAPTER ACTIVITY

1. Lay out the Astro Wheel and read each placement in relation to your life or someone close to you. Notice how the cards interact with each other. Which cards are in the center? Do they relate to any cards around them?
2. Lay out the Celtic Cross Spread on you or someone you know. Without asking any questions, see if you can determine the overall important theme right now

by looking for repeating numbers, repeating suits etc. Notice what card 3 is saying, as that is why you asked the "question". Since we asked no question, this will represent what should have been asked as it is prominent in the person's life right now. Cards 1 and 2 give information as a whole or are a miniature of the entire spread.

CHAPTER 7
Mediumship Reading

Often, I find that clients will book a tarot reading, but really want a mediumship session. They may not know what to ask for, and if this happens, you can still give a mediumship reading without being a medium. That is the great thing about tarot. It will help you answer anything. Let's get into this.

If you do not have medium skills (or maybe you just feel uncomfortable or insecure about your abilities and are not ready to share them) but want to read for someone who is requesting this service, I offer two methods in this chapter that will help you give an accurate mediumship reading. Tarot can open the door to get the session started, and you can add to the information if something intuitive comes to you.

METHOD ONE FOR A MEDIUMSHIP READING

This is highly useful when you are not expecting to do mediumship and are put on the spot in the middle of a reading. Lay out the cards in this 5 card Spirit Spread.

Spirit Spread On The Fly

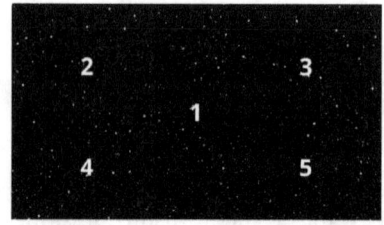

1 - Represents the spirit/loved one - who they are

2 - Another identifier of the spirit and who they are

3 - What they want you to know in relation to them

4 - A message for your life right now

5 - A second message for your life right now

More cards can be drawn for each of the positions to add more information to the reading.

METHOD TWO FOR A MEDIUMSHIP READING

If you are already expecting to do mediumship, you can prepare ahead of time for a more detailed reading. Using Court Cards will help you identify the spirit, giving you the astrology sign, whether they are male or female, a child, young adult or adult. Picking a card from the rest of the deck can tell you when they passed. I would refer to the Chapter 11 on timing and use Major Arcana to represent years instead of months (the Fool can represent someone who has just passed recently, although the Wand cards can tell you one day etc. The World can mean 21 years ago or more. If the person you are reading for is 20 years old, this is someone who passed just prior to their death).

*Begin by removing the Court Cards from the deck t*o make two stacks of cards. When you are ready to start, shuffle both and deal one card from the top of the Court Cards stack. This will represent the person trying to come through for your client. Read the card to gain information about the person. You can add any of your own intuitive thoughts, as well.

Next, spread out the cards from the second stack (the rest of the deck containing the four suits and Major Arcana) and ask questions. Draw a card for each answer.

Example 1:

1. Interpretation of the loved one or the person who is coming to visit: Queen of Pentacles. This is a female. She is an Earth sign or has characteristics of an earth sign. She could be Taurus (or whatever sign you programmed this card to represent). She is good with money or handling money, down-to-earth and generous. Or money issues before passing. It could even be an indirect message that something with money is coming up after her passing, such as an inheritance or they left unpaid bills behind, etc. (Here are the keywords of Queen of Pentacles from my first book: A woman in control of finances. A dark haired, dark-eyed woman who is good-hearted, down-to-earth and practical. Methodical, yet easy-going, she is an extremely good business woman who can be very helpful to others. A woman offering you a business opportunity. She is good with money management.

Can be a good patron. A very established person, with big bucks. Honest and reliable. Can place a false value on money, making it the main focus of life. A tendency toward materialism. A woman who marries for money.)
2. This description has told you a lot about the person. For more details about this person, you will use the second stack of cards. Spread them out, ask a question in your mind and draw one. Then relate these details to the client.

Question #1 – How long ago did this person pass?

A Major Arcana card would suggest years. The Heirophant 5 would be five years ago.

Question #2 – What was this person's personality like?

The 7 of Swords. This suggests sneakiness. Maybe this person was someone they had issues with, like an ex or a sibling they didn't get along with, etc. Read your keywords assigned to this card. Also, the sword suit can help. This was a person who was rational; relied on thinking. Since this is a more negative card, maybe they had mental issues or disorders such as narcissistic, or they were always in their head, etc. (If a blatantly negative card comes up, it is trying to tell you something. I know that I always think sweet loving Grandma is going to come in, but that is not always the case. Some souls that had a bad relationship with the querent come in to make amends or be forgiven.)

Question #3 – Did this person pass over peacefully?

5 of Cups. This card shows grieving. It suggests that the person was not ready for death. They have regrets shown here with the figure looking at the spilled cups of wine. They need to realize there are two cups still standing and move forward over the bridge to their new life. Possibly they are still stuck in this dimension because they are locked into an emotion or haven't crossed over, or they are not moving on because they had a difficult relationship with the client and want to resolve it first (as shown in the 7 of Swords).

Question #4 – How did they die?

3 of Swords. This card could literally be heart issues. Or the swords could indicate mental issues. Maybe taking one's own life from a broken heart. You could also look at Chapter One relating to health questions. This could relate to Quadrant 3, or if the color red is standing out it would most likely be a heart or cardio-vascular issue.

*(At this point, the reading is getting fairly negative. You always want to leave the session on a positive note for the client. This can be done by giving them the opportunity to resolve the issues with this person and let go. Or by bringing in other family members who can offer support by drawing more cards to see who else is wanting to visit.)

Question #5 – Has this person been around the client or trying to get their attention?

10 of Cups. I would answer this as a "yes", meaning they have been around the client, and the client has probably noticed this... or they will in the future...since this has a blue background.

The client may have their own questions such as, "Does this person know I love them?" Answer in the way that is most comfortable for you, or draw another card.

    3. And now for the really cool part - getting the first letter of the name. There are 22 Major Arcana cards. They are assigned here in numbered order with the corresponding letters of the alphabet (I used the English alphabet here, but substitute your own). Magician 1 is A, High Priestess 2 is B, Empress 3 is C and so on. When you get to the end,

you will lump together U,V,W as U is uncommon and will most likely be a V or W. But all three of these letters are similar to each other so you will be getting close enough. They will be represented by World 21. Skip X as it is not often used, and lump Y with Z as The Fool 0 - which is also related to 22, so it will be the last card.

1 Magician A	12 Hanged Man L
2 High Priestess B	13 Death - M
3 Empress C	14 Temperance N
4 Emperor D	15 Devil - O
5 Heirophant E	16 Tower - P
6 Lovers F	17 Star - Q
7 Chariot G	18 Moon - R
8 Strength H	19 Sun - S
9 Hermit I	20 Judgement - T
10 Wheel J	21 World U,V,W
11 Justice K	22 Fool Y, Z

You should still have two stacks of cards – the Court Cards and the rest of the deck. Put the Court Cards to the side, and deal from the top of the other stack, until one of the Major Arcana comes up to represent a letter.

You could even try to spell out a name or the initials. If you are spelling out a name, I would add the letter X to 22. This may not always work if you try to spell out the name because sometimes spirit talks to you in sounds rather than spelling. I got a female spirit, MEH, which to me would mean a name starting with that sound "meh". Megan, Melanie, Melissa etc. Sometimes the spirit is giving the name of someone they left behind they are still concerned about, such as a child or family member. You will have to consult the cards for more information or ask "yes" or "no" questions to determine if this is their own name or they are referring to someone else. Ask your client how they know the person. Sibling? Child? Classmate? Coworker? Aunt?

What is the letter of the first name?

The Emperor 4

The letter "D".
Choose more cards as needed for letters.

From here you could go back to the Court Card stack and draw again, to indicate another spirit coming to visit.

Example 2:

From the Court Card Stack: Page of Swords. This would represent a child in the astrology air sign suit, Gemini, Aquarius or Libra. A smart child, bright, quick mind. Possibly dark hair and eyes.

Example 3:

From the Court Card Stack: Knight of Pentacles. This would represent a young adult – someone age 30 or younger. Red or blonde hair (can be dyed) green or blue eyes, someone with a lot of energy, creativity.

Example of a Reading

Here is a reading I did for myself:

The Spirit:

The person coming through is a female. Lighter hair, hazel eyes. Emotional. Kind-hearted. A water Sign.

Question #1 – How long ago did this person pass?

Over 21 years ago.

Question #2 – What was this person's personality like?

Optimistic, outgoing, creative.

. . .

Question #3 – Did this person pass over peacefully?

Yes. As a child. Happy.

Question #4 – How did they die?

In bed. Possibly illness.

. . .

Question #5 – Has this person been around me or trying to get my attention?

No. Possibly going to the person still grieving.

What is the letter of the first name?

The letter "M".

I felt like the "M" represented "Mary". I tried to think of someone I knew with that name that had passed away over twenty-one years ago but could think of no one other than an aunt named "Mary Margaret". But some of the details didn't make sense, and I didn't have a way to verify.

I asked for the second letter.

The letter "E".

"Mary Esther" popped in my head. This is my sister's first and middle name. But she is still alive.

I picked another letter.

The letter "H".

Results:
MEH. I had the intuitive feeling that this was the sound of the name. Since intuitively I had gotten "Mary". I was still feeling "Mary Esther" and that the spirit was someone that I know well. I asked if this was Mary's daughter, and I got a "yes" card. Her name was Elizabeth. She passed twenty-four years ago (World card). She died as a child, and was found in her crib (9 of Swords). She is a water sign (Queen of Cups - both Elizabeth and Mary are Cancer water signs). She has never tried to appear to me before (5 of Cups) but rather is spending her time with the ones still grieving. I think Elizabeth was giving me a description of herself that I could pass on to Mary of what she looks like now. Then I decided to stop and chat a little more with her. I shared the information with my sister who really needed to hear it.

END OF CHAPTER ACTIVITY

Practice trying to contact someone specific that you know details about that can be verified. This will help you ascertain if that is who is actually communicating with you, rather than trying to figure it out blindly. For example, if your mother has passed and you want to talk with her, schedule a time when you are going to do the reading (if you let them know ahead of time, they are more likely to show and this will make it easier for you). Ask for her to come in for a visit. Lay out the cards. See if they reflect your mother. If not, decipher who it is paying you a visit.

CHAPTER 8

My Secret - How to Answer a "Yes/No" Question

Sometimes it is easiest just to get a quick answer on something, especially when you are pressed for time or don't have the energy to go through a long or involved spread.

The key to getting a "yes" or "no" answer lies with programming your deck ahead of time. I talk about this in book one. And this programming is as simple as choosing cards to represent "yes" or "no", as well as "maybe" or "undecided/unknown".

I will share with you here the cards I have assigned these meanings, but I encourage you to *choose your own*. The rest of the cards in the deck can act as "maybe" or add more information to the "yes" or "no".

These cards mean "yes" to me:
    Empress
    Sun
    World
    The 4 Aces
    9 of Cups
    10 of Cups

These cards mean "no".
    3 Swords
    Death
    Tower
    Devil
    5 Cups
    5 Swords
    7 Swords

'FOOL' PROOF TAROT

This card means "unknown":
   High Priestess

This card means "undecided":
  5 of Wands

If none of these cards comes up it means "maybe".

MAKING "YES" AND "NO" ANSWERS HAPPEN FOR YOU

Go through your deck and decide which cards have a decidedly negative tone, and which evoke an unquestionable feel-good energy. Assign these to mean "yes" or "no" respectively. This makes getting an answer easier, because you will remember which cards you specifically like and don't like. You will never have to question whether they are a "yes" or "no". And trust that these cards will answer for you. If one of your "no" cards turn up, for example, it does in fact mean "no".

For "undecided", maybe you decide to choose the 7 of Cups or the Moon card. When "undecided" is the answer, then something else has to come into play to turn the answer toward a "yes" or "no". Or it could mean there is no definitive answer.

For example:
Question - Will this job make me happy?
Answer: "Undecided/maybe". This can mean there are things about it that could make you happy, and aspects that could make you unhappy. So, this is a neutral answer. However, you will want to look and see if the job could make you happy at a later date, since the "unknown" card can mean that a missing piece of the puzzle has not yet arrived. You start the job, are happy with your co-workers but not happy with the pay. This is a "maybe" in relation to your happiness with that job. It is partial happiness. But in the future the boss gives everyone raises, so now you're happy, and your "maybe" answer has become a "yes".

For the "Unknown" answer (High Priestess or your choice), this means that there is no set path or future. You are in unknown territory. Even the Universe does not know the answer.

If your answers seem to be off or inconsistent, check for interference by simply asking if the answer was interfered with. If so, you will have to do something to clear yourself and your space.

Examples of a Yes/No Reading

Will I be getting a job soon? (I usually pick 4 or 5 cards in a group.)

This would be a "yes" as the Empress has shown up. The other cards can give more information, such as the Wheel meaning the job pops up out of the blue and is a good thing. The 6 of Cups someone from the past offers the job or it is emotionally fulfilling. Knight of Cups could mean starting at ground level in pay but something with potential.

Will I meet a boyfriend soon?

"Undecided" with the 5 of Wands. Something else has to come into play, before this will become a "yes" or "no".

Is taking this trip a good idea right now?

None of the "yes", "no" or "undecided" cards have come up, so the answer is "maybe" or neutral. It doesn't matter either way if you take this trip or stay home. It is not a significant influence in your life.

Does this man love me?

The World and Ace of Cups are saying, "Yes."

Same question – Does this man love me?

There isn't a definite "yes" or "no" here. Maybe this person thinks they love you, but don't really understand what love is. Or maybe it is still in the developing stages since the Prince of Cups has an offering of love. The answer is "maybe".

Does this man love me?

The Devil and Death cards say, "No."

Does this man love me?

High Priestess says, "Unknown," meaning there are no answers to this question at this time. Maybe he will develop love or maybe it will go south, but not even the Universe knows right now. Note there are also no Cup cards which could signify love.

Is this man good for me?

We have "yes" and "no" cards coming up, the Sun and 5 of Cups. So, some of the qualities about this man are good for you, and some are not.

END OF CHAPTER ACTIVITY

1. Decide what cards in the deck mean "yes", "no", "undecided" and "unknown" to you.
2. Come up with a variety of "yes" and "no" formatted questions and practice getting familiar with your cards that mean "yes" or "no".
3. Practice bringing the "yes and no" format into your other readings. You can use a "yes or no" anytime you have doubts or are unsure about what a reading is saying.

CHAPTER 9

New Year or Birthday Readings

This is a popular reading to offer for New Years, birthdays or anytime of the year. In astrology, the birthday is the personal new year. It is common for emotional issues to come up just prior to the birthday, as well as an increase in problems, that usually die down after the birthday passes. Almost as if you are clearing out whatever has not been dealt with and cleaning the slate for another year. Let's get into year-long readings.

The national holiday of New Year's does affect you because the year number changes. If you study numerology, you will see the huge effect numbers have on your life. This is because the numbers are a symbol carrying the vibration of the planets. This could also be related to the matrix code, if you are one of those persons willing to go down that rabbit hole. But if you study numbers, it becomes undeniable the influence they have.

For example, as I write this it is 2021. The number 21 is success and liberation after overcoming trials. The number 20 is the awakening and realizing you are a spiritual being. If you deny this truth, life is much more difficult. You can see that reflected in the year 2020. Many people awakened spiritually and otherwise. It was unprecedented in the challenges and changes presented to the population worldwide with Covid and the questioning of power structures. Things we never thought would happen, did happen. The imagery for 20 is the dead awakening and rising from their graves.

Like previous chapters, the handy Astro Wheel is helpful for setting up the new year reading. To set it up for the New Year, card 1 would be January, card 2 February and so on. For a birthday, you would start with card 1 being the month of the birthday.

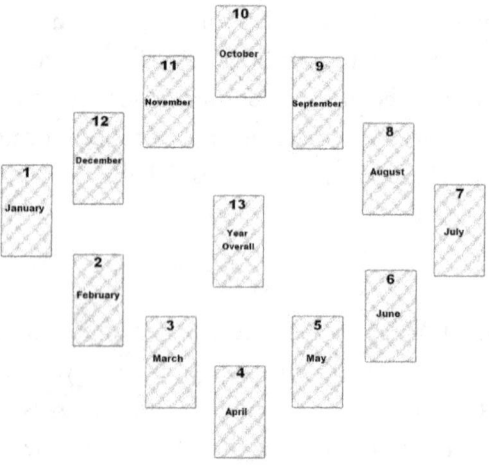

If you follow astrology, it may be beneficial to read the planets connected to the Astro Wheel spread. For example, if someone has a 4 card (such as 4 of Cups) in the 8th position, then Uranus might be having an influence in that area of their life (relating to

Uranus in the 8th House for an astrologer). This area of the 8th position is other people's money, taxes, legal issues, death, mediumship and the other side and soulmates from previous lifetimes. Uranus is sudden shocking or unpredictable changes. So, a Uranus card in the 8th position could point to sudden changes in a legal or court case, the signing of a contract, appearance or departure of a soulmate etc.

Look to the nature of the card to see if the shocking change is positive or negative. The imagery on 4 of Cups is positive. The hand of god holding out a gift to the individual. It comes out of nowhere. Just like Uranus energy. This could be in the emotional or romantic realm because it is cups. So, this could refer to the 8th house of the appearance of a soulmate, or a marriage contract (legal issues). You can even look at that single cup being offered as the Ace of Cups, and the three cups grouped together as the 3 of Cups. So, these two cards are related to the 4 of Cups. They mean new relationship and celebrating good news.

Numbers and the Planets:
   1 – Sun
   2 – Moon
   3 – Jupiter
   4 – Uranus or Rahu (north node or dragon's head)
   5 – Mercury
   6 – Venus
   7 – Neptune or Ketu (south node dragon's tail)
   8 – Saturn
   9 – Mars

For more astrology/tarot information, see Chapter 13.

END OF CHAPTER ACTIVITY

1. Do the Astro Wheel spread for your coming year, beginning with the current month you are in. Lay out each card to represent consecutive months. See if there is accuracy in what material you are dealing with each month and use the card warnings to change any negatives before they happen.
2. You can also do this for the next twelve days. This will be a faster tracking method and will help you learn to interpret the cards based on your experiences. Take notes on your daily cards at the end of each day.

CHAPTER 10

Suicide, Demon Possession & Reading Interference

If you are unaware of or do not believe in negative entities, it doesn't mean your clients share that same opinion. Many may come in asking for help because they have had an unexplainable experience. Telling them what they are seeing, hearing or experiencing is not really there isn't going to help the situation and may lead to more problems for the person. They may even contemplate suicide. Let's get into this uncomfortable topic.

Regardless of your beliefs, you need to validate the person coming to you for advice and help. There is much going on in the world that we are unaware of, and people are dealing with the pressures of feeling out of control. This can lead to serious contemplations or actions as a result. Never mind the entities that may be attaching to people and giving their influence toward these negative directions. Call it what you will. Maybe you like to think of it as influence from negative people, or negative thinking instead of entities. Either way, we have a problem, Houston.

ANMARIE UBER

SUICIDAL CLIENTS AND LOVED ONES LEFT BEHIND

At some point you will have to address the difficult topic of suicide when doing readings. Either the person or a family member is suicidal, or they are a loved one left behind and struggling to deal with another's suicide. If it is the former and you are not a spiritual or professional counselor, I would recommend you leave the session on an uplifting note and refer them to professional help. And offer a suicide hotline number they can call. It is always wise to keep this number or other helpful referral numbers handy, when presented with these situations.

It will be up to you to gauge it, depending on what the person says. Sometimes they are just depressed and need to have a deeper understanding of their life and purpose. This can sometimes be enough to someone snap out of a depressed mindset.

When reading for the loved one left behind, it is helpful to affirm that they are not responsible for the suicidal person's actions and that everyone goes when it is their time. They will feel guilt, even when it is not warranted. But the guilt helps no one. Guide them to work through this and see it from another perspective. And find what the gift or blessing is that came out of this horrific experience.

POSSESSIONS AND ATTACHMENTS

Many times, a client can come in, and you feel the dark or negative energy emanating from them. Sometimes it comes up in the reading. This could be due to a number of things, but the main ones are: being in an environment of negativity, having attachments or partial to full possession.

Environmental: A client can have a very downer-type energy because they are surrounded by or living with negative people who are adversely affecting their energy field by association and close proximity. They may be surrounded by family, co-workers or a significant other - psychic vampires who have energy attachments. These can be caused by a variety of reasons, such as heavy drug use, delving in ritualistic magic, inheriting demonic spirits through the family line, etc. What is recommended is for the person to have a clearing session and extricate themselves from the people/source of the problem.

Attachments: If the client has attachments (this is common), many times they are aware of this – they hear voices talking in their head which are not their own. They feel compelled to do things out of character etc. The entity can come through a portal in their auric field when the subject is weak. Most commonly this could be from any drug use related to altering the brain (antidepressants, hallucinogenics, etc.) whether prescription or illegal, surgeries where the body was cut, being in low energy environments, trauma to the body, and many other causes/scenarios. A problem of attachment should become readily apparent in a reading. If the entity is hiding or trying to disguise its presence – and influencing the reading – the Moon and Devil cards will come up together in the same spread or layout. This is a signal of psychic interference, and the cards should be reshuffled and cleared, or you should switch to a new deck.

Partial Possessions: Sometimes an entity has gained further access to the individual beyond just an attachment. They should be referred out to someone who deals with that type of removal.

Possessions: People that are truly possessed could come in as a client, although it does not occur very often. There will be a marked difference to the session, and you should end the reading as soon as you can. This person will usually say disturbing things, and/or your intuitive antennae will pick up that something is terribly wrong. It is always important to stay out of a person's energy field as there are legions of minions connected to the main entity possession. Wear protective crystals, essential oils or other tools to keep your energy field strong and block them from attaching to you. I do not recommend attempting to help a person who is possessed, as their soul is usually long gone.

HOW TO CHECK FOR INTERFERENCE IN A READING

Simply ask with a "yes or no" reading if you are in doubt or questioning the answers you are getting. Disruptive and whacko answers signify interference. A reading that brings you down and has a very heavy feel is usually interference. And as mentioned, the Devil and Moon will come up together in a spread when a dark entity is trying to interfere with the reading. The Devil is a good card to have in the deck, because it seems to come up without fail when there are negative forces at play.

GREAT WAYS TO PROTECT YOURSELF DURING SESSIONS

- Frankincense essential oil on body points of entry (wrists, between shoulder blades, back of neck, low back, first chakra area, center of the forehead and above the naval).
- Burning frankincense resin incense, white copal resin incense, sage, etc.
- Wearing or having crystals in your vicinity such as sugilite, turquoise with a copper vein matrix running through the stone, black tourmaline and other black stones. Forming a grid of crystals around where you are sitting is also helpful.
- If you are already in a room with a possessed person and don't have protection, visualize a bubble around you and push outward when something tries to attach

to you. Put a mirror on the outside reflected back and get out of the room as soon as possible, as it will take focus to maintain the bubble.
- Finally, salt is one of the best defenses against something trying to attach. Rub it directly on to the area of the body where you feel an invasion.

Above all, do not project fear. These are low-level bottom feeders who are no match for a soul being. But again, unless you are skilled in this area, leave it alone. The consequences of going against them are not worth it, as you will suffer if you hold any fear in your life. Fear gives them the upper hand – you gave your power over to them. And since they work in secret and behind the scenes hiding themselves (they have to hide and trick because they are weak), you have to discover and learn their game first before you can hope to defeat or rid yourself of these evil annoyances.

END OF CHAPTER ACTIVITY

1. Read up on some of these issues and become informed. Don't leave yourself defenseless. Don't let these people into your house.
2. Have crystals or other protective items ready to use in every session.
3. Create a list of people you can refer the client to who handle the types of situations listed in this chapter.
4. If you don't believe in negative entities or that they can mess with you, consider opening your mind and testing the waters. (No disrespect, but this belief that they don't exist unless you believe they do is usually a coping method due to fear, or a false "new age" narrative you bought into.) Read other people's accounts or testimonies and come to your own conclusions.

CHAPTER 11
Nailing Down Timing

This is an interesting thing...timing. I do feel that we are shifting into a phase of time where this is harder than ever to predict. I used to be able to predict timing with extreme accuracy. Now it if one tries to read out further than ten days to two weeks it becomes very difficult. (If you want to get down the rabbit hole on what is happening with time, you may want to check out my YT fringe channel.) I am hoping this phase changes soon.

Having said the above, I do think you should continue to try to predict timing, and there are several ways to do this.

PREDICTING TIMING – SIMPLE METHOD 1

Assign the Major Arcana as months, the wands as days, the cups as weeks, and the swords and pentacles as months. People cards (Court Cards) mean a person is responsible for the timing. An example: 3 of cups means 3 weeks; 4 of wands means 4 days; The High Priestess means 2 months; Queen of Wands means the person represented by the card is determining when it will happen.

PREDICTING TIMING – DETAILED METHOD 2

The first thing to do is get familiar with the suits and how they relate to the elements and seasons.
Each suit is related to an element:
Wands – Fire
Cups – Water
Swords – Air
Pentacles - Earth

Each suit is also connected to astrology, which connects it to the seasons. The Sun follows a path through the seasons, and it is mapped by the equinoxes and solstices. The astrology cardinal sign of each element starts off a season:
Aries – Spring – Fire (Wands)
Cancer – Summer – Water (Cups)
Libra – Fall – Air (Swords)
Capricorn – Winter – Earth (Pentacles)

- Wands – Spring

- Cups – Summer

- Swords – Fall

- Pentacles – Winter

When you are reading on timing, the faster moving elements relate to a shorter period. Wands are fire. Fire burns quickly. It represents days. Water moves but in a more meandering fashion.

It represents weeks. Swords and Pentacles are slower energy and represent months.

Putting this all together:
    Wands – Spring – Days
    Cups – Summer – Weeks
    Swords – Fall – Months
    Pentacles – Winter – Months

The number on the card represents *how many* days, weeks, months.

There are three categories of cards you will pick: Major Arcana, Minor Arcana (the four suits of 1 - 10) and Court Cards (People Cards – Page, Knight, Queen, King). How you read timing will depend on which of these you pick.

    1. The Minor Arcana Suit Cards

If you pick a suit card, numbered 1 – 10, you will use the timing connected to the suits. For example, I want to know when I will meet a partner. I pick 5 of Wands. That card means spring and/or 5 days. Here is exactly how you will read this:

Begin with today's date. If spring is in 5 days from the present, then your answer for timing is 5 days. If spring does not occur in 5 days from the present date, then you will read the 5 as representing the calendar month (May the 5th month), so you will meet them the following May.

2. The Major Arcana Cards

We also have Major Arcana in the deck that do not have a suit. The cards 1 Magician - 12 Hanged Man represent the respective calendar months January to December. The cards 13 Death - 21 World represent months (13 Death is 13 months, 14 Temperance is 14 months, 21 World is 21 months or a year and 9 months - anything beyond that gets difficult to read as things change).

The 0 Fool Card means the timing is anytime. Sooner than 1 month, or immediately.

Here is exactly how you will read Major Arcana cards for timing:

Begin with today's date. You draw the 8 Strength card. The timing is in August. Or you pick the 18 Moon card. The timing is in 18 months.

3. Court Cards

That leaves Court Cards. Since they have no number, these cards defer timing over to a person. A person influences the timing. That could be you or someone else. The person determines when the timing of an event will happen. Or a person has to make a decision before the event can happen. It is not on a set timing, but up to a person. If a Page card comes up, it means children are involved in the decision-making of the timing. Perhaps you are planning to move but need to find out first what area has a good schooling system for your children. Or you need to wait until their present school year is over before moving.

Let's put this into practice and read on the timing of an event.

Example 1: The date today is March 12th 2021. The person wants to know when they will start making better money. A card is drawn: The 6 of Swords. Swords is fall. Is fall 6 months after March 12? Six months from March 12 is September. You will need to look to see when the Fall Equinox is, as it is usually somewhere between September 21 – 23. The fall equinox for September 2021 is the 22nd. So, the answer is "no" – in 6 months it will not be fall. It will still be summer. (Each new season begins on an Equinox or Solstice. For reading timing according to seasons, spring starts March 20 on the Spring Equinox. If the date is March 19, it is still considered winter.)
Since the answer is "no", the 6 of Swords would be read for the number 6 as the calendar month which is June. So, this person's money will increase in June.

Example 2: Using the same information, the person wants to know when they will start making better money. The date is March 12th 2021. You draw the 10 of Pentacles. Pentacles represents winter. In 10 months from March 12th will it be winter? Ten months would be January, so the answer is "yes". Your money will get better in 10 months. For a more detailed answer, pick a second card. If you pick a "2" card, this means your money gets better in 10 months and 2 days.

Example 3: Using the same information, you pick the Queen of Cups. The answer to timing is up to the person represented by the Queen of Cups.

Example 4: Using the same example, you pick the 4 Emperor card. The timing is April.

Example 5: Using the same example, you pick 16 The

Tower card. The timing is 16 months, or 1 year and 4 months.

If you are ever in doubt about an answer, you can always refer to Chapter 8 and ask a yes or no question such as, "Is this timing correct?" You can also ask if the timing can be moved up sooner. Remember practice makes perfect. The more you use this method, the faster you will get at reading the timing.

END OF CHAPTER ACTIVITY

1. Decide how you are going to program your cards first before you use them for timing. You can assign them with time periods like I have suggested in this chapter or come up with your own.
2. Practice timing certain events. Read for yourself concerning something you want to bring into your life and ask for the timing of "when" this is likely to happen. Use method 1 or 2 to predict it. Take notes. Did this happen when I thought it would? If not, did something change, or did I change the outcome by my thinking, decisions, attitudes?

CHAPTER 12

How to Read Reversals – Easy Peasy

Reversed cards (cards that appear upside-down when you lay them out) are generally accepted as a signal that the interpretation of the card is changing or different somehow. Reading reversed cards is a choice. If you don't want to bother with them, turn all the cards upright and read as normal. You will still be accurate, as there are enough challenging cards in the deck that can replace a reversal.

If you want to include reversals in your readings, it does not have to be overwhelming. You do not need an instructional booklet to refer to. You do not have to learn seventy-eight new meanings. Just choose one or more of these handy tools and reading reversals will become second nature.

Here are several options or suggestions:

- A reversed card could be signaling *an area of concern or something that needs to change in order to bring out the best meaning or strength of the card.* What needs attention? What needs to be transformed? What is the cause of issue? The key point of the reading – area of focus, turning point. A reversal signifies an important card. Working on this card can heal the problem. An answer to what needs to be done or the cause of the problem. All cards have the potential to be positive so the goal here is to alter your perception, change something you are doing or work on an area represented by the card to bring out the more fortunate qualities and therefore change the outcome of the reading.

Interpretation using a relationship reading: Let's say you are doing a relationship reading, and the 4 of Pentacles is reversed, landing in the partner position. It tells you the partner needs to address the content this card reflects. Four of Pentacles attitudes could be causing issues, and signals what needs to be transformed to improve the relationship or secure its future. And possibly to change the energy of that Death card if it is in the outcome position. So, 4 of Pentacles indicates holding on to money. Being miserly. Fearful of money. This issue is affecting the relationship, and the party responsible (your partner) needs to heal their approach and attitude to money. Maybe they are keeping money from you, hiding it, not contributing their fair share, expecting you to give up things you shouldn't have to, etc. The positive aspects of 4 of Pentacles could be moving to a new place or working in a bigger city to make more money. Or having a lot of money. But even though positive, since it is reversed, it is still the cause of an issue in the relationship.

- A reversed card can be read as a slightly more or less meaning of the card. So, if it is the Sun card reversed, the card would not be as positive as the Sun upright. But still positive. If it is the Devil card reversed, the normal negative effects of the Devil are not as pronounced. So, a negative card becomes more positive, or its effects lessened, and a positive card becomes slightly less positive. This will be solely based on your reactions to each card and whether they feel positive or negative. If it is a neutral card and reversed, the effects or benefits of the card are going toward the negative. Or the card itself is becoming more negative – playing out a negative aspect.

Interpretation using a relationship reading: If you read reversals in this way, the Four of Pentacles could be taking on an even more extreme version of miserliness, to the detriment of the relationship reading. Or a move to a city for money reasons could break apart the couple.

- A reversed card could signal that you should look for connected cards to this one. For example, let's say you have the 10 of Wands and 3 of Pentacles reversed. You would look for other cards that are numbered 3 or 10 or other Wand and Pentacle cards. Or cards that have the same imagery or coloring as the reversed cards. These connected cards may be of significant importance and need attention in order to affect the outcome or improve the situation.

Interpretation using a relationship reading: Reading reversals in this way, we find that the 4 of Pentacles is connected to the 4 of Cups and the Death card, all being fours. It is also connected to the 2 of Pentacles, being of the same suit. Or maybe you see a connection between the yellow color in all the images. Or that the individual is sitting in both of cards 2 and 5. Or even Death sitting on the horse. Etc. These cards would be read as "connected".

If you decide to connect the numbered cards – all the fours – Then problems with holding on to money creates a problem seen in the 4 of Cups of not valuing the love that you have. Or being too caught up in the relationship to see the love potential. This leads to the last "4" card of Death. Which signifies an ending followed by a new beginning. That ending could be positive (transformative) for the relationship or negative (the end of the relationship). So, the connections with all three of the cards needs to be addressed.

If you decide to connect the 4 of Pentacles to the 2 of Pentacles, because of shared suit, this can mean the up and down of money and holding on too tightly are both affecting the relationship. Or maybe taking on a second job (2 of Pentacles) will help with the counting pennies or miserliness energy of the 4 of Pentacles.

- A reversed card could signal a way out of the current circumstances. Or a new way of looking at something. Also, turning things upside-down to see from someone else's perspective or look at things in another way. See the other person's point of view.

Interpretation using a relationship reading: The 4 of Pentacles could be signaling seeing your money situation with new eyes, or in a different way. Instead of feeling like you don't have enough or fear the loss of money, instead see how abundant you are. Since this is a relationship reading, you may want to try and see things through the eyes of the partner. Or figure out the problems related to the 4 of Pentacles. It may give you deeper insight and understanding into the other person and affect your lives for the better. If there are relationship problems, the way out could be moving to a bigger city to increase your income.

. . .

Again, it is recommended to choose only one of these ways of reading reversals, or at the maximum two, until you get well versed in doing this and can switch back and forth as desired.

END OF CHAPTER ACTIVITY

1. Decide whether you are going to use reversals when you read.
2. Decide which method(s) you are going to use to read reversals and lay out the cards in a spread of your choice. Practice interpreting the reversals in relation to the entire spread.
3. Come up with your own way of interpreting reversals.

CHAPTER 13
Astrology & Numerology Connections

Learning numerology and astrology has added to my tarot practice and brought a detailed richness to the readings. I highly encourage any student of tarot (as we all are) to study these sciences. Whether its western or eastern astrology, Pythagorean or Chaldean numerology etc. find something you enjoy and add it to your tarot card reading. So, let's get to it...some astrology and numerology connections with the cards...

Want to get super detailed in your readings and blow the client's mind? Following are two methods of bringing astrology and numerology into your readings for even more accuracy.

FINDING ASTROLOGY SIGNS IN TAROT

Many have opinions on which Major Arcana cards relate to what an astrology sign or planet, but this is subject to interpretation, as there is no set assignation, which can make reading with astrology very frustrating. Much less trying to use the Minor Arcana, as well. (There is a very involved system which breaks up each degree of an astrology house with a planet/sign correlation that can be assigned to a card, but that is for another day). Remember that trump tarot cards were put into a 22-card format in Marseille, France and modern cards follow that same format. It has been proven that it is not related to the tree of life or the letters of the Hebrew alphabet. Rather, it was a choice, so that card decks would be unified for publishing to the masses. The cards were originally connected to Christianity and showed different aspects of a person's spiritual development. The Christian virtues such as charity and hope were assigned to specific cards. These early decks had more than forty trump cards (Major Arcana – the name given later on) and none of the early decks were complete. My guess is they had 52 cards to match the 52 weeks in a year mapped by the Chaldeans. So, the 22 cards have no bearing whatsoever. In fact, Waite switched the 8th and 11th cards (making Strength the 8th and Justice the 11th) to force them to match closer to the 22 letters, as well as adding much symbolism in the imagery relating to the cult group in which he was involved.

Unless a creator of a deck has assigned specific astrology to a card (such as adding the symbols in the picture), you are on your own in choosing what resonates with you. Because let's be honest, if the High Priestess relates to the moon and we have a Moon card, which is it? Trying to apply astrology to the cards is a difficult task, even for those who know astrology well. I am going to show you the best way to use the signs first. And then an easy way to use the planets to gain more information from a reading.

The best way to use astrology signs with tarot is in the interpretation of the Court Cards. These tend to be more difficult for many to interpret and are not numbered. In my first book, you will see that these cards are actually very easy to read.

Astrology Signs all have a planet connected to them, so it is helpful to learn both. If you can't remember the characteristics of a sign, you may remember the characteristics of a planet.

In astrology you have an element and a quality.
    Elements: air, fire, water, earth (sound familiar?)
    Qualities: Mutable, Fixed, Cardinal

I have divided the Court Cards into the signs connected to the elements.
    Cups is water – Scorpio, Pisces, Cancer
    Wands is fire – Aries, Sagittarius, Leo
    Swords is air – Gemini, Aquarius, Libra
    Pentacles is earth – Taurus, Capricorn, Virgo

The people (Court) cards would be assigned as follows:

- Pages – children in those signs. Page of cups would be Scorpio, Pisces or Cancer children and so on.

- Knights – young adults in those signs. Knight of Wands would be Aries, Sagittarius or Leo etc.

- Queen – An adult person in those signs displaying feminine qualities.

- King – An adult person in those signs displaying masculine qualities.

So how do you know which sign represents the card? I chose to use the qualities for this. The Kings are cardinal, the Queens are fixed, the Knights are mutable. Each suit is related to a season, and there is a sign at the beginning of each season marked by an Equinox or Solstice. (Aries marks the beginning of the Spring Equinox. Aries is fire/wands. It is cardinal which means it takes action and leads. Therefore the King of Wands is Aries.)

Note: It may be helpful to actually write the astrology symbol or word on a card so you will remember in the beginning.

NUMBERS AND THE PLANETS

We have been talking about the zodiac signs. Now let's talk about the planets. An easy way to assign a card to a planet is by using the nine numbers found in the deck. Every card has a number value (minus the Court Cards – although they could be given a sequential order such as 11, 12, 13, 14) and the numbers all add to 1-9. So, a compound number such as The Star card 17 would be an 8, because 1+7=8. Learning the 9 numbers in relation to planets is very easy. Each number relates to a planet, and indirectly to the zodiac sign it rules. The North and South Nodes are included here from the old system.

Planets in relation to Chaldean Numbers

- 1 - The Sun - Leo
- 2 - The Moon - Cancer
- 3 - Jupiter - Sagittarius (secondary Pisces)
- 4 - Uranus, North Node - Aquarius
- 5 - Mercury - Gemini, Virgo
- 6 - Venus - Taurus, Libra
- 7 - Neptune, South Node - Pisces
- 8 - Saturn - Capricorn (Secondary Aquarius)
- 9 - Mars - Scorpio, Aries

- The Sun is the overall character, career and how this person shines.

- The Moon is emotional needs and how we nurture.

- Jupiter is expansiveness or contraction. Increase.

- Uranus is shocking unconventional upsets. Unpredictability.

- North Node – What you should be doing in this life, but it is so new to you as a soul that you don't always see it.

- Mercury – Movement, changeable, never stagnant.

- Venus – How we love, what we value, different types of love.

- Neptune – How we dream or imagine. How we can deceive ourselves.

- South Node – What you were naturally good at in past lives but need to leave behind as it will not necessarily bring you success this time around. What comes easy. Turning to the past for answers that are not there.

- Saturn – Hardships, areas where fear will trip you up. Karma.

- Mars – Drive, passion energy. What excites and motivates you. Action to take.

This is an interesting study to see how a planetary influence can affect a card with the corresponding number. You may have your own way of relating planets to the cards, such as Uranus being connected to the Tower because of the electricity and sudden impacts. But it can be both. The Tower can be Neptune (7) and Uranus if you like. These are just suggestions.

END OF CHAPTER ACTIVITY

1. Write a list of all the planets and signs with their symbols. Get familiar with the symbols.
2. Get your astrology chart printed and learn where the signs and planets are in your chart. Astro.com has a free chart service under free charts – you want the natal and/or ascendant chart. Find your Sun Sign card (significator) in the deck.
3. Find out the Sun Sign of your family, friends or those close to you. Study the common ground characteristics you notice between all the Geminis, all the Scorpios etc. Learning about yourself and those close to you will help you learn astrology. You will be looking for patterns.
4. Learn the elements of the signs. This will give you general information – you learn all twelve signs by only learning four elements. For example, you learn about the water element. Now you know something about Scorpios, Pisceans and Cancers. If you are really motivated, learn the opposite signs and the qualities to get a feel of how the signs interact with each other.
5. Write down keywords for the planets and their nature. Write down keywords for each of the zodiac signs.

CHAPTER 14
Card Symmetry

Reading tarot cards is like trying to piece together a puzzle. You look at the cards not only by themselves, but how they interact as a unit. People who are really good at reading patterns can use a layout or spread of tarot as just that – a pattern. Let's get into some obvious connections the cards are making to each other.

When you lay out tarot cards, they begin to interact with each other. This communication is shown in patterns through the symbols of the cards by numbers, colors, imagery, suits, meanings etc. Through this, some cards are specifically connected to others. The symmetry of the whole is what gives a much more detailed picture. Astrology is similar. You can look at each planet and the sign it is in, but add that to the house location and you have three pieces of information that give more details. Looking at each planet in this way gives a lot of details about each puzzle piece. But when you put all of it together and see how these pieces interact (aspects), you get the individual's whole horoscope picture.

. . .

Here are some of the things to look for, in deciphering how the cards may be speaking to each other using a four-card spread:

- They share the same number.

The 3 of Swords and 3 of Pentacles are connected by number and relate to one another.

- The number on one card references the spread position of another card.

The 3 of Swords is connected to the third card the 8 of Pentacles.

- A color is prominent and noticeable in 2 or more cards.

The color blue stands out in Card 1 and 4. These are connected.

- They share the same suit.

Card 1 is connected to card 4 because they are both swords.

- The interpretations/meanings are connected.

Example 1: Here we have three cards with similar meanings. The three, five and seven of swords all allude to someone lying, cheating or hurting us in some way and stand out.

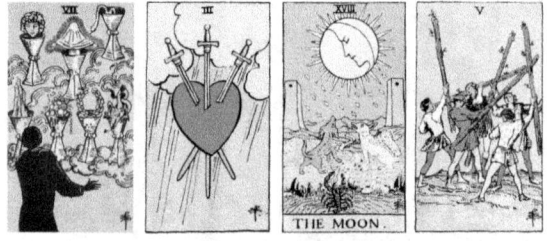

Example 2: Here we have three cards with similar meanings, the Moon, 7 of Cups and 5 of Wands all alluding to confusion and answers not being clear.

Example 3: Here we have the 5 of Pentacles and 8 of Swords both meaning ungrounded fears about money, or believing that you don't have what you need. These two cards are connected to each other.

Example 4: The Hanged Man and 2 of Swords show an inability to move forward. The 9 of Wands could be interpreted in the same way. These three cards are connected by similar meanings.

- The cards show a progression of an event.

The 5, 7 and 9 of wands show a progression of a battle, to gaining ground in the battle to wounded after the battle. These cards are connected through progression of a battle.

The Lovers and Devil both show Adam and Eve. In love and happy, then progressing to feeling trapped in the relationship. These cards are connected through progression of a relationship.

- The cards share the same image.

The 2 of Swords and 8 of Swords both have figures wearing a blindfold. These cards are connected and bringing out the importance of the blindfold.

- Two figures in a card are looking at or away from each other.

We have 2 Knights on a collision course with each other. Or maybe the Knight of Cups is moving toward the figure in the 8 of Swords, but the Knight of Swords is in the way. Or the Knight of Swords has left behind the figure in the 8 of Swords to go after the Knight of Cups.

. . .

End of Chapter Activity

1. What are other ways you see different cards connected to each other?
2. How can you use the symbology of the cards to enrich your readings?

CHAPTER 15
Major Arcana as Spiritual Archetypes

The tarot cards originally had more than 22 Major Arcana called Trumps or Triumphs. They focused on the spiritual aspirations and challenges of life. Many see the Fool to the World card as the Fool's journey back to the soul, progressing through each of the cards on the way. It can represent the cycle of reincarnation or breaking that cycle.

You can be at any stage of these 22 cards. It is not necessarily a linear progression, as you may find yourself dealing with Sun card material, and the next week Death card material. They can be related to psychology, archetypes, astrology or whatever helps you identify with the card.

A great way to use them is for contemplation. Pull one card a day that you are drawn to and see how it is playing out in your life. Look for connections between the cards, such as all of the "one" numbers – Magician 1, Wheel 10 and Sun 19. Are they showing different levels of progression or devolvement? Note the connections in a journal and leave room for logging future thoughts. For example, the Lovers card 6 and the Devil card 15 show Adam and Eve in two different scenarios. Are they progressing toward or away from a certain outcome. Where did they lose their way spiritually to go from Lovers to Devil? Relate your findings to your own life. Did you enter into a relationship thinking the partner was a blessing, when they were actually something else, altogether. Notice the patterns in the imagery. How things seem to advance forward or retract. See where you are replaying patterns or getting caught in looping traps.

A card can be laid out to represent what stage you are currently in. Remember the Major Arcana are not always linear, and can go in reverse, so you can be at any stage.

There are several books that already cover this type of study, so I won't repeat this here. For a deeper dive of the cards, you can start with the book, "Jung and Tarot".

END OF CHAPTER ACTIVITY

1. Lay out the Major Arcana cards in order and see if you notice your own life in the cards. Which ones does your soul relate to? Which one feels like a stage in life you are going through now? Which ones bring up fear? Fear is the only thing that holds you back. And what process can lead you to the ultimate liberation goal of reaching the World and Fool?
2. Pick up a few books that resonate with you and do a more in-depth study of the cards.

CHAPTER 16
Additional Keywords & Symbology for the Major Arcana

In my first book I discussed programming your deck. One way of doing this is giving assigned meanings to the cards using keywords or phrases. This helps you remember the card, without having to use a reference booklet. I listed several key words to choose from in that book. Here are some *alternative* meanings to add to those but as always, use what resonates with you.

I am also listing some of the symbolism in the cards. There is a much deeper story to these, but that is not subject matter for this book, as the symbolism may be upsetting to many about the true nature of our reality and its rulers. I do hint at some of it here. The Major Arcana are tributes to or triumphs of the gods. Remember the creator and artist of the Rider Waite deck were both involved in the Golden Order of the Dawn, and the cards are heavy with old symbolism. However, I do feel these symbols were once positive, but have been hijacked. Use the cards for your own purposes, not what some order or group wants to make them.

Fool

THE FOOL.

Foolish, younger person (Emperor older person), child, grandchild, selfish, immature, young soul, the world is your oyster, you are protected.

Symbolism: The zero is formless. Beginning of the god force into physical form. Knapsack is the subconscious mind. White flower symbolizes purity. White Sun is the god force. Dog is loyalty. Curly red feather is Osiris cult. Anubis is hinted at by the appearance of the dog warning Osiris. Up on a mountain like the Hermit and related.

Magician

Manifester. Mirroring another's behavior or projecting. Standing your ground. You have everything you need.

Symbolism: The male priest. Virgin male. I am that I am starting point. Hands as above so below. The scroll is phallic. The belt is a serpent full circle representing the zero space, time and kundalini. White tunic is purity, red cloak is the physical life force and material world. The four elements are on the table of the wizard. Lilies hearing Spirit and roses desires of life. The lemniscate above his head represents infinite knowledge. It also represents karma and the endless time loop of reincarnation. Constraints of time and space. Spirit trapped in matter. Adam.

High Priestess

THE HIGH PRIESTESS.

Major psychic gifts, having a good memory, holding secrets.

Symbolism: Female counterpart to the Magician (he is conscious, she is unconscious mind – however this was originally the female pope "Papess" related to the Pope card 5 now called Heirophant.) The virgin female. Eve. Crescent moon under her feet and cycles of the moon on her crown. The cross is matter (Earth). The pomegranates and palm leaves on the veil behind her are female ovaries and phallic male. Canopy is veiling other worlds. The two columns are Boaz feminine and Jacin masculine – the names given to the two main pillars of the temple in Jerusalem and from Solomon's temple. They are the two pillars in the Tree of Life Kabbalah. Hebrew mysticism. They also represent a mystery of opposites. She holds the torah. Cult of Isis – Isis deity with moon crown. Her dress becomes water.

Empress

Feminine nature, promised land, flourishing with life.

Symbolism: This is the pregnant mother. Creativity and never-ending flow. Streams of consciousness symbolized by the water flowing. Wheat growing in the foreground is abundance. Twelve stars represent twelve tribes and twelve zodiac signs and is a nod that she is a deity - the symbol on the heart stone is Venus or Aphrodite. Her scepter represents royalty that rules over the common folk. Bloodlines. The crest originally held by the Empress (now replaced by Venus stone) beheld a phoenix, signifying Horus and the Temple of the Phoenix. The Phoenix was the creator of reality and a self-made being. A deity of the Sun, rebirth and creation. This is Isis in her role as Hathor, Lady love - an Egyptian goddess and sky deity, goddess of the stars (the Queen of Heaven), fertility, motherhood, the symbolic mother of the pharaohs who were representatives of Earth. The Hathor race are from the planet Venus.

Emperor

Father figure, older person, old soul.

Symbolism: He is holding the staff of life and the world. An old ruler connected to an old civilization on Mars possibly destroyed by war. He has armor on under his red clothing, the red color of Mars. The goat on the throne is a nod to the worship of the goat god and that he is a deity – Mars god of war. The crown reaffirms this. It can also be seen as Aries which is the sign ruled by Mars. The ram and Ramses. The old deck shows a character similar to the Empress, in the temple of the Phoenix . He is the counterpart to the Empress.

Heirophant

Training, learning something new, passing an exam, gaining wisdom.

Symbolism: The 3-level scepter is supposed to represent the holy trinity but since this was originally The Pope card, this is symbolizing the Vatican. The three levels of rule. The keys on the box at the bottom of the card are the keys to the illusions and mysteries. Exoteric and esoteric. Possibly the keys to the box or cube that makes up the matrix illusion. The on/off switch. He is the gatekeeper. The 3-level crown is shown on the Vatican flag with the two keys. Red is physical world. The pillars are represented here again as in the High Priestess card. This is a different faction of ruler. The two acolytes are guards to the temple with a "Y" on their backs is the two paths. Also, the finger of the god, being marked, destiny determined by this god. The hieroglyph for the letter "Y" is a reed. This refers to the "field of reeds" – a heavenly paradise where Osiris rules. The crown is symbolizing this is a deity. He does not have a lemniscate but it is represented here by the stole around his neck. The figure eight represented by ribbons. Reincarnation cycle but also so much more.

Lovers

The ultimate Soulmate, wanting to hold on to innocence.

Symbolism: Adam and Eve with Archangel Raphael. Making contracts with angelic beings and pulled into a loop or cycle. Tree of flames – the twelve signs of the zodiac. The red wings a demon spirit or angel, with the serpent on the tree and the flames of hell. This card leads to the Devil card. A creation of Adam and Eve and the altering of the DNA. Relating back to the High Priestess who is Isis and Eve.

Chariot

Good opportunities coming which lead to greater things, Charging forward.

Symbolism: An Egyptian Sun deity. A charioteer god. He wears a sun crown. A canopy of stars above him and wings on the chariot which signifies travel from an air vehicle. This could also relate to Mercury or other chariot gods. The winged orb is knowledge and a symbol of Isis. They are also on the helmet of the Knight of Cups. The symbol below it on the shield is man and woman coming together. The white and black sphinxes is the light and dark working together controlled by a higher puppeteer or in this case steered by the charioteer through destiny and the life script. Astrology also tells the tale of life scripts. The half-moons on his shoulder pads suggest a connection again back to Isis and The High Priestess, as well as Hathor (estate of Horus – Osiris) Selene the moon goddess, Helios the sun charioteer etc. Astrology symbols on his belt, magical or alchemical symbols on his skirt. This god seems like a summation of all the sky gods, as the sun/stars, moon and four pillars of the chariot are represented here. The god of the script. The canopy of stars behind him suggests portals, visitors from somewhere else, able to travel through the stars and chariots or ships used by the gods such as U.F.O.s.

Strength

Having courage, giving inspiration and encouragement.

Symbolism: The enchantress. A female master between this world and the next. A physical adept (adept originally meant "one who has gained knowledge of alchemy, the occult, hermetic philosophy and magic). Initiates in the Egyptian mysteries could walk among the lions and not be harmed if they kept their sexual energy in a virgin-like state. The lion symbolizes the sexual nature but also one of the ruling factions defeating another (as shown in the World card – the four factions in the corners of the card showing who has control of which area of the world). The white dress symbolizes purity. The lemniscate is matching the one in the Magician card. Rulers of time.

Hermit

Heading in the right direction. Your soul is lighting the way.

Symbolism: His staff is connected to the wands suit. The light in his lantern is a six-pointed star. Spirit encased in matter. The six-pointed star is associated with Saturn worship. Six triangles is the Egyptian hieroglyphic for the land of the spirits. It is used as the ancient Egyptian Seal of Solomon and the reincarnation of Horus in a physical body. The six-pointed star is an ancient Chaldean seal believed to represent a deity. So, in this case we have no crown but the star possibly representing Horus the god of the sky. And other Greek, Roman etc. gods that follow. Horus of two horizons. Evening and setting Sun. A Sun god or the evening star. Right eye morning star. Left eye evening star. The lantern is in the right hand.

Wheel of Fortune

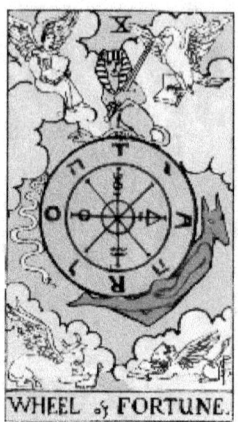

Blessings are coming. Taking a chance. It is your lucky day.

Symbolism: There is a lot going on in this card. It shows the small circle in the center of the Earth. Concentric circles of the realities existing around us, as shown on old maps. The cross dividing the Earth into sections, each ruled by one of the four shown in the corners. These are supposedly the 4 fixed astrology signs, but Aquarius is depicted as an angel. This is the angelic realm, or possibly something we are unaware unless indoctrinated into their mysteries, the temple of the Phoenix on upper right is represented, the bull god in lower left and the lion god usually depicted as a serpent with a lion's head or Yaldabaoth. The four players in the game. Gods of the underworld below, with the red Anubis and gods of the light above. Whose turn is it to rule the Earth? The spin of the wheel of karma will tell. Each has a copy of the script. Each god in the corners has a Hebrew letter assigned to it as seen on the outer wheel. Together they are YHVH (Yod Heh Vau Heh) the unpronounceable name of god. There are also the letters "taro" alluding to the High Priestess card and the Torah. But also hidden meanings. And the word is an anagram sentence: Rota Taro Orat Tora Ator. The wheel (rota – rotate) of tarot (taro) speaks (orat – orate) the law (tora – torah) of Ator (possibly Hathor which is Osiris). The alchemical symbols in the middle wheel represent mercury, sulphur, water and salt. Creation of life/death and coded human DNA. The sphinx is found on masonic temples all over the world, and there are multiple sphinx stone remnants being discovered all over the Earth – not just in Egypt.

Justice

Clarity to see the truth, Ending old karma.

Symbolism: Anubis god of the dead is often depicted holding the scales of justice. This can be attributed to later gods in other cultures as well, with different names but representing the same persona or person reincarnated. If one is unjust, the punishment can be death. There is a crown on the head, so this is definitely a god/deity. We see again the two pillars represented in the High Priestess and Heirophant cards. Sword is up related to Arthurian sword Excalibur in the Ace of Swords, and the sword of life of the ruler. The scales relate to karma and reincarnation loops. He is dressed in red like the Heirophant. The religion is connected to the law. Worship of gods. Also wearing the stole or ribbon of reincarnation loop. The veil between lifetimes, but also the old laws that we are unaware of but are operating under. The veil hides the true rulers of this world. The image of Justice was originally a woman wearing a blindfold and can mean impartiality.

Hanged Man

Release the old to allow in the new.

Symbolism: Stuck in the upside-down world. God of the underworld ruling. This is the deity in control represented by the halo around the head. The antichrist. The pose of Judas. Jesus replaces Judas becoming the twelfth. Christ/antichrist. Related to magnetism. Magnetism is what occurs but is mistaken for gravity. Magnetism holds everything together. Time makes it move or gives motion. Linear time which stand still but seems to move. Time requires sacrifice. The reset of the game or ages. Sands of time running out. Twelve is the magnetic element. The magnets create the toroidal field we are in. The tau or "T" shaped cross is used in ancient Egyptian Mithraic initiations. Lineage of the

Christ deity. The blue and the red. The two warring factions. Blue blood. Red blood.

Death

Shedding your old identity and ways of relating, letting go of control.

Symbolism: The rose on the flag is Arthurian, Rosicrucian, alchemical, golden dawn. All connected to the bloodline royal factions. One faction conquering another. Curly red feather Osiris cult and related to the Fool card, Knight of Swords and the Knight of Wands. This can be related to the Grim Reaper, but it is one of the four horsemen of the Apocalypse. The first horseman rides a pale horse and is conquest, war and the antichrist. The fourth horse is pale, ridden by Death and represents pestilence and disease. The Egyptian god Resheph is represented as the deity of war, plague and disease. The book "Behold a Pale Horse". Black armor symbolizes new life under new rule. The Pope here relates back to the Heirophant card. The pillars from the Heirophant, High Priestess and Justice are seen in the background with the sun coming up. A new sun god to rule. Images come to mind from the pillars of Tor and the Arthurian theme which is all interconnected. The dead rule. The soulless ones of Isis.

Temperance

Brain waves, thought forms, waves of interference, breaking out of mind programs, wait for the right time.

Symbolism: The iris flower can symbolize the goddess Iris. This is Archangel Michael. The cups pouring back and forth represent repeated time loops and the manipulation of time. It also represents alchemy – changing one substance into another and manipulation of the conscious and unconscious mind. He is a solar deity or represents the sun god with the symbol for the sun on his forehead – the pineal, third eye and all-knowing. The sun or one-eye capping the pyramid is in the background. Pyramid inside of a cube represents spirit trapped in matter. The foot in water and one on land signifies immortality, the elixir of life and nectar of the gods.

. . .

Devil

Mental illness, seeing no way out, trapped, facing your demons, possession.

Symbolism: This is Baphomet or the goat gods of luciferianism, satanism or whatever they want to call worship of the demon gods. It is shown on the thrones of the Emperor and King and Queen of Pentacles. This is Adam and Eve who have grown horns and a tail and worship the beast. The inverted star represents the goat god, and human turned away from their divine self. The soul is gone and the demon takes over. The Chitauri that Credo Mutwa mentioned before his death that live underground. The creature ties victims to itself while it is sick. As it becomes better, it releases the human victims and then chases them, flying to capture the prey. The adrenaline rush in the blood feeds the creature.

Tower

Changes in real estate, job/career or residence. Feeling broken or in shock.

Symbolism: Changing of the guard. Who will be the ruler from the Wheel and World card (the four factions)? A crown is blood. Which bloodline of the rulers will take over? You see the crown falling from the top of the tower (connected to the cards with the towers) and the lightning bolt of another god conquering this one. The Tower of Babel. You see the "yahs" in the sky representing the Egyptian moon god relating to Yahweh and back to the Wheel of Fortune card. They are also seen in the Ace of Swords card. Adam and Eve consumed with money and desires of the material world are seen here falling from the tower.

Star

Potential, being recognized for something or having star-quality.

Symbolism: The goddess of the lake (lady of the lake in Arthurian). Relating to the Temperance card. Alchemy. A god of the water and land. The gods are represented in the background sky. The five ripples of water are the five dimensions humans are encased in, and the five streams of water the five senses of human. The ibis bird is a symbol of Thoth, the god of the moon, as this image is at night. A giant goddess. The Egyptian goddess Efnet was associated with both the moon and sun. She represented moisture as a lunar goddess, and dryness as a solar goddess. The bird could also be a Bennu, a red and gold solar or flame colored bird. This bird was a symbol of resurrection and represented a deity that was a self-created being. It represented the Sun, birth and creation. The picture in this card hints at creation, and of course a "star" is a sun. The Bennu is related to the phoenix.

Moon

Hiding your light, what is hidden will be revealed, hormonal fluctuations.

Symbolism: Once again the two towers as seen in other cards. The "yahs" as seen in other cards. In old decks droplets of blood, signifying sacrifice and the bloodlines. One is a werewolf, the other a dog. Both forms of gods of the underworld. Anubis is suggested here with the dog, and Wepwawet by the wolf. The Sun and Moon god represented here. The crayfish is the Egyptian scarab Khepri the scarab faced Sun God – he who cometh forth – god of rebirth and return of the sun.

Sun

A bright future, having a lot of energy, positivity brings success.

Symbolism: The Sun and sunflowers relate to the twin gods Nut and Geb who birthed the sun gods. One is the sky and the other is land. This also represents Castor and Pollux. And the birth of the sun god. The child is wearing a crown. The birth of the Christ. Gray horse can signify false light.

Judgement

Decisions around legal documents coming to a close, resurrecting something from the past.

Symbolism: This is the Age of Aquarius, the second coming of Christ and Angel Gabriel announcing the second coming of Christ. A double ten means time speeding up. The cross is earthly life. It is also the Swiss cross of the ruling families of ancient pharaoh bloodlines. The horn is related to the Sun and is the Egyptian symbol of resurrection and rebirth, which is what you see happening here. The resurrection of the dead. Or dead walking. The controlling family bloodlines ruling over the common folk. Calling you through the tunnel of light to be reincarnated over and over. Trapped or lured into the cycle like the pied piper.

Worship of the god(s).

World

Life comes full circle, good luck.

Symbolism: The wreath symbolizes a world subjected to time loops, reincarnation. This garland of leaves is representing the serpent eating its tail. Law of rebirth and karma. No beginning or end. The trap of the world. The trap of time. The Hanged Man pose of the central figure is a sacrifice to time. This being is a hermaphrodite – both man and woman. The four figures in the corners are supposed to represent the four astrology fixed signs, but they represent factions and the areas they rule. Two of the light and two of the dark. Players in the game. The four god aspects or four cornerstones relate to, "I have", "I will", "I know", "I desire". The purple drape represents enlightenment. Magic wands masculine energy.

CHAPTER 17

Additional Keywords & Symbology for the Cups Suit

In my first book I discussed programming your deck. One way of doing this is giving assigned meanings to the cards using keywords or phrases. This helps you remember the card, without having to use a reference booklet. I listed several key words to choose from in that book. Here are some *alternative* meanings to add to those but as always, use what resonates with you.

Here are the meanings for the cup cards:

Ace of Cups

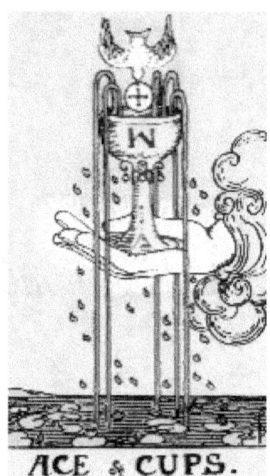

Success in love, abundance. Waters of life feeding the emotions.

Symbolism: The Holy Grail. The five streams of water are the five physical senses. The Catholic chalice holding the blood of Christ. The Holy Eucharist is over the cup symbolizing the Catholic host of the body of the Christ. The Holy Spirit descending is symbolized by the dove. The spirit into flesh and blood. A being taking over a body. The nectar of the gods. Water lilies and lily pads representing a symbol of unity for the nation to ancient Egyptians. It was also a symbol of rebirth. The W is west and reversed is East or "M". M is a destructive deity. Possibly of sunrise and sunset. This could be the obvious, M is moon and W is woman, but I doubt this is the case. I would be interested in hearing from you, if you have research to share about the W and M. What I think it is...the Egyptian hieroglyph letter M is represented as an owl, which is the symbol of darkness, death and celebrated dark qualities. Used by the illuminati, freemasons, and many other groups which base their origins in the ancient Egyptian rites. Here we see it reversed as W, which symbolizes new life. The W is the hieroglyph of a quail chick. The X on the host is similar again the symbol for the Royal Arch – see 3 of Pentacles. X represents a basket or chalice. Here we see the host of the Catholic church kept in a Tabernacle with the symbol for the chalice on it and the ritual of the Royal Arch, the chalice again holds the blood of Christ. The host is his body.

Two of Cups

A committed love or relationship.

Symbolism: This is yin and yang. Archangel Raphael is shown as the angel of the south. Although this can be seen as Yaldabaoth the serpent with the lion head. The lion ruling faction. Drinking the blood or nectar given to gods. The caduceus is the medical symbol but has connections to the kundalini. Also, the DNA strand and the creation of Adam and Eve, who could be represented here as humankind. They are wearing crowns which would suggest the toasting of two gods coming together. The two warring factions working together. A wand with serpents and wings is a magic wand and used in alchemy. Alchemy of male and female. The caduceus is applied to chevrons which are used by the ruling elite bloodlines. It can represent the entity taking over the body of a human.

Three of Cups

Celebration of an anniversary, well wishes, toast to the future, good orators or public speakers.

Symbolism: The trinity. The triple goddess. Hecate. The charities. The seasons. The moirai. This also celebrates Isis, Osiris and Horus. The three colored garments are different aspects of the sun goddess.

Four of Cups

A decision needs to be made around a relationship. Grounding yourself from becoming too emotional. Seeking enlightenment.

Symbolism: Green is envy and dissatisfaction. The Holy Grail being offered. The Bodhi Tree that Buddha sat under to gain enlightenment.

Five of Cups

Grieving the past, needing to step into the future, two significant people one a soulmate, the other a bridge that leads to them.

Symbolism: The black cloak is grieving. Blood has been spilled. The bridge to the other world.

Six of Cups

Family, secrets in the family, someone in the family not being honest. A memory of a pure relationship.

Symbolism: The freemasonry "X" carved into the stone is the symbol for Osiris and sex rituals. What it is doing on this card I don't want to speculate. This is a "6" card and the X resonates to 600. X is the mark of death, and a falling cross, a sign of the antichrist. The castle in the background adds to the feel of blood-line families and Osiris illuminati worship for a very long time. The white lilies suggest innocence of childhood and the essence of children. The taller child is wearing a hat similar to the couple in the 3 of Pentacles.

Seven of Cups

Dishonesty and lying, not able to see the future, thinking with the mind/ego instead of the intuition/heart.

Symbolism: All that is offered to someone who undergoes the initiation rites, you can have everything the world has to offer. A partner, castle, jewels, victory and success. He is turned toward the right. This is the left-hand path. Denying going within. The figure with the sheet over it is your inner self.

Eight of Cups

Walking away from a significant relationship.

Symbolism: Red shirt is seeking desires in a different place. The beach or shore is a place between dimensions.

Nine of Cups

Achieving a goal, the finish line, dreams fulfilled.

Symbolism: The feast of Osiris. The red plume a nod to this god. The blue tablecloth with chalices symbolizes blue blood.

Ten of Cups

Happiness and celebration, things better than you thought they would be.

Symbolism: Rainbow is a promise from God. Freemason Order of the Rainbow – an international secret fraternal organization for teenage girls. Implies the pot of gold. A true sign of magic and mind control.

Page of Cups

(Pages usually mean a message or a child but here are general meanings.) A good dancer or actor. Secrets revealed. Someone with unconventional ways of doing things.

Symbolism: The fleur-de-lis on his shirt is Calvinism which is Freemasonry Sun worship. The fish symbolizes the Piscean age and the time period of Pisces.

Knight of Cups

(Knights usually represent a young adult or situation.) Someone who gives from the heart. Someone bringing good advice.

Symbolism: The winged orb is a symbol of Isis worship. A winged sun or disc is divinity royalty and power. One of the four horsemen of the apocalypse. Wings on the heel can represent Mercury, although with the garment of fish this is also related to the Egyptian fish god Rem.

Queen of Cups

Someone with unique and powerful psychic gifts. Someone who appreciates art or stands apart from a crowd. Personal magnetism.

Symbolism: She is holding a very unique cup. It has winged beings that resemble the Ark of the Covenant from Solomon's Temple. It is viewed by some as a type of weapon of extraterrestrial origin. Sea or water nymphs can be seen on her throne as merbabies. She is the fish goddess or Egyptian Hatmehyt – "she who is in front of the fishes" - and offers life and protection. In Greek she is Amphitrite, wife of Poseidon, as seen by the King of Cups.

King of Cups

Someone with deep intuitive knowledge. A good advisor. Having a hidden romantic nature.

Symbolism: The fish around his neck hints that this is King Neptune or Poseidon which is the Egyptian god Yam, or Dagon the fish god merman. Robe of gold with blue is the master of his fates in freemasonry, and the gold chain is a freemason grand officer.

CHAPTER 18
Additional Keywords & Symbology for the Swords Suit

In my first book I discussed programming your deck. One way of doing this is giving assigned meanings to the cards using keywords or phrases. This helps you remember the card, without having to use a reference booklet. I listed several key words to choose from in that book. Here are some *alternative* meanings to add to those but as always, use what resonates with you.

Here are the meanings for the sword cards:

Ace of Swords

Victory. Success in a big way. Standing your ground.

Symbolism: Excalibur the sacred sword. Yahs are emanating from around the hilt depicting the Egyptian moon god. Laurel leaves and an olive branch on the crown signify victory. Egyptians used bay leaves to symbolize victory and to crown a hero. Isis who is also Athena, discovered olive oil. The olive branch represented hope, prosperity, peace, glory, victory and purity. King Poseidon (King of Cups) stuck his trident in a rock and a salty spring burst forth, symbolizing power. We can see the correlation here to Excalibur being stuck in a rock, and the person with power/next to be in power could remove it – Arthur.

Two of Swords

Decisions coming up. Walking on eggshells or a fine line. Future unclear.

Symbolism: The blindfold is connected to the 8 of Swords and the Justice card. In the mystery schools of Ancient Egypt and in Freemasonry a candidate for initiation was blindfolded to represent a state of darkness before emerging into the light of knowledge when the blindfold was removed. This implies some type of ritual connected to the card and the "X" pose as described in the 6 of Cups. A freemasonry gesture to indicate someone has reached a certain level of initiation. The crescent moon is a symbol of death and rebirth, as signified with the blindfold. Once the mysteries are revealed, life is never the same. It is also the ability to see through the veils of the High Priestess and Justice cards. The water represents welled up emotion that the person cannot face.

Three of Swords

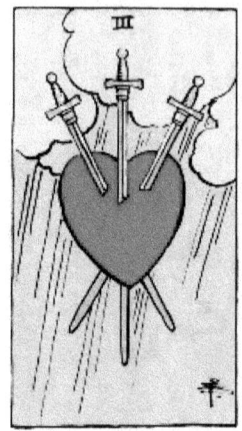

A stormy relationship. Broken relationship. Dark night of the soul. Hurtful words.

Symbolism: Ancient Egyptians believed that the heart represented consciousness and was the center of life itself. They did not remove the hear during mummification so that it could be given back to the deceased in the afterlife. This can represent the death of the soul, or the trinity god.

Four of Swords

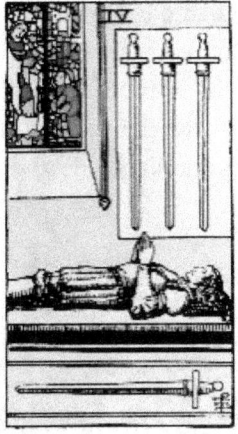

Have patience. Opportunity is coming. Need to put something to rest or put an end to something. Hiding from the world.

Symbolism: Here we have a Templar knight with the Excalibur below on the tombstone. The sword is the key to the Holy Grail and its protection. The swords of King Arthur and his men had an equal cross as did the Knights Templar. This is the Swiss cross relating back to the ancient pharaoh bloodlines still ruling today. The Catholic Church is connected to these bloodlines, rituals, symbology and ceremonies, and the knight here has his hands in prayer. The stained-glass window appears to be from one of the large cathedrals in Europe where the templar knight's tombs are found. See the 5 of Pentacles for a further description of the stained-glass window. In the window it appears to be a seated figure on a throne with a castle or archway in the background (see the Ace or 3 of Pentacles for a description of arch) and a person at their feet in a pose of supplication. The letters PAX are above the head of the individual on the throne, written inside a halo above the head. PAX is insinuating some type of secret ritual here taking place in masonic and other orders, that is outwardly shown to the public as taking the body and blood of

Christ at mass – the host and chalice shown in the Ace of Cups. The PAX symbol is often seen with other symbols such as the dove (Ace of Cups) and an olive branch (Ace of Swords). A PAX is a small flat tablet adorned with a sacred image that worshipers kiss when offered the kiss of peace. The man on his knees in the window reminds me of the Heirophant card of the Pope on his throne and two acolytes kneeling beneath him.

Five of Swords

Choose your battles, need to know when to quit, may need to give up or walk away. Or someone is walking away from you. Selfishness.

Symbolism: The harsh clouds represent the sharp energy of the card. The green cloak is avarice. This scene can be showing the defeat of the Knights Templar.

Six of Swords

A need to move forward, or things finally moving forward. Leaving and not looking back.

Symbolism: This is the Egyptian ferryman Mahaf, who carried the souls of the deceased into the underworld. He also was a herald who announced the arrival of the pharaoh to the sun god Ra, who merged with Osiris the god of the underworld. Other ferrymen of souls can be represented here, such as Charon. The choppy water in the foreground symbolizes a change from consciousness to the smooth water of unconscious. The wand of the ferryman symbolizes Egyptian magic.

Seven of Swords

Remembering hurts from the past, going camping, leaving a group or community of people, moving forward with hard lessons learned.

Symbolism: Ancient tents were used and called tabernacles. The literal meaning being "dwelling place" used by the Torah's priests to describe YHWH's tent shrine Inside the Tabernacle tent there is a curtain behind which is the Holy of Holies where the Ark of the Covenant was to rest. The tabernacle symbolically mirrored the cosmos. The entrance faced the rising sun and a lamp was placed where the seven planets visible to the human eye – of which there are seven. This relates to the number of this card. The planks of the tent are made of acacia wood. A courtyard is in front with a large sacrificial altar. The Tabernacle and Ark of the Covenant are built by two craftsmen. One who's name is Bezalel (which is oddly similar to the name of Bezaliel, the 13th watcher of the twenty leaders of two-hundred fallen angels and is called the Shadow of god). The Tabernacle was meant to be a movable dwelling for YHWH so sacrifices could be continued. It was half the size of the Temple of Solomon. The god El and other deities were known to live in tents. There are remains of the Tent of

Hathor dedicated to the Egyptian goddess also known as Isis. The colors were gold and red. The Ark and other "holy" relics could be weapons of the gods.

The hat reminds me of a Shriner who are a secret masonic society – the "Ancient Egyptian Arabic Order of Nobles of the Mystic Shrine". In the background of this image there is what appears to be a ritual going on.

Eight of Swords

A controlling person or being controlled. Tied up in your own thought prisons.

Symbolism: The blindfold is connected to the 2 of Swords – see description there. The loosely wrapped linens around this person's middle suggests of Egyptian mummy before burial. Also, the binding of the arms. Definitely related to initiation rites connected to death. This appears to be the mummy bindings coming off after death and transitioning to resurrection and new life.

. . .

Nine of Swords

Depression. Worry. Revelations in the night. The planets in astrology. Mind programs. Attachments.

Symbolism: The bedspread has astrology symbols and roses in the patchwork. The white and red rose represent the two competing sides. The rose to ancient Egypt had healing properties. It can represent that in this image, as well as earthly desires as seen in other cards with roses.

Ten of Swords

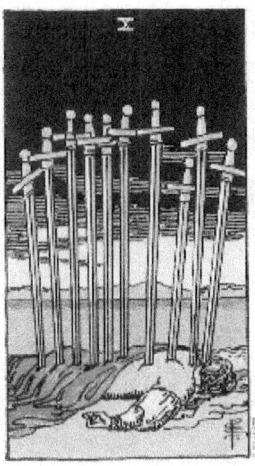

Putting an end to a bad situation. Assassination of character, or in extreme cases actual assassination. Overburdened with other people's thoughts and opinions.

Page of Swords – (Pages usually mean a message or a child but here are general meanings.) Resolve. Empowered. Sticking to the truth.

Symbolism: Here the swords are inserted along the spine. In ancient Egypt the spine represented stability and towers (as seen in other tarot cards) represented this stability. It related to the god Osiris and his spine. The sky in the background can be seen lifting into sunrise, as the horizon chases out the blackness.

Page of Swords

(Pages usually mean a message or a child but here are general meanings.) Standing up for a cause. Ready to swing and fight.

Symbolism: He has gone up high to an area of mental clarity. This feels like the battle in the heavens of gods against angels, and possibly one of the archangel warriors.

Knight of Swords

(Knights usually represent a young adult or situation.) Charging forward to resolve a problem. Leading a cause.

Symbolism: Related to the Death card with the red feather and pale horse. One of the four horsemen of the apocalypse. Also related to the Mars god. The butterflies on the harness represent the air sylphs but also allude to the horse as a flying machine or chariot of the gods.

ANMARIE UBER

Queen of Swords

A person who welcomes truth. A guarded but welcoming attitude. A mental battle of wits. Someone who can hold their own.

Symbolism: She is wearing a crown which signifies a deity. It is made of butterflies which suggest the elemental sylphs of the air element, as does the butterflies and winged cherub on her throne. This hints again at a flying being. If we look at the image on the throne, we see a similarity to the winged orb on the Knight of Cups helmet, and on the front of the Chariot card 7. This is a nod to Isis, who had magical abilities and could grow wings to fly. She is high up in the air in this image suggested by the clouds on her cape and close to her in the sky. The butterfly is related to the Egyptians wrapping and mummifying the dead like a chrysalis so the person can emerge immortal as the butterfly after death. This is an immortal deity, and possibly Isis. Also seen in Japanese mythology as Amaterasu who brought darkness to the Earth and was banished from heaven to the Earth. She was given the Sword of the Gathering Clouds of Heaven. This is also in Egyptian mythology the ruthless warrior goddess Sekhmet. The frayed ties around her wrists suggest her breaking free of her bloodlust and saving humanity from her darkness and punishments. Justice and balance existed once again on Earth. The sword held upright is connected to the Justice card and the seeking of justice. In the center of the throne you can see what appears to be a crescent moon, but it looks more like the cruel sickle curved sword of the Egyptians with a handle.

King of Swords

A person forging a new way of thought or thinking. Someone who argues or likes to fight. A highly analytical mind.

Symbolism: On the back of his throne there are butterflies, two Egyptian curved sickle sword with a handle and a small winged air elemental sylph over his shoulder. This suggests once again a deity with a crown and a flying vehicle. He is also high up in the air like the Queen. He is an aspect of the god Ptah and consort to Sekhmet in the form of the god of use of will and using thought to bring the world into existence. The creator in heaven. Conceiving by thought and realized by the Word. This is represented here with the swords suit of air and mental thought.

CHAPTER 19
Additional Keywords & Symbology for the Wands Suit

In my first book I discussed programming your deck. One way of doing this is giving assigned meanings to the cards using keywords or phrases. This helps you remember the card, without having to use a reference booklet. I listed several key words to choose from in that book. Here are some *alternative* meanings to add to those but as always, use what resonates with you.

Here are the meanings for the wand cards:

Ace of Wands

Success over struggle, a new idea that changes everything, a change in rulership or power. Opportunities for advancement. The laborer card. Enterprise.

Symbolism: The hand of god coming out of a cloud holding a club. Meaning the beginning principle, origin or starting point. The leaves symbolize new growth.

Two of Wands

A blessed individual. Unlimited opportunities. Looking to or reading the future.

Symbolism: At the ledge of a castle. The cross of lilies and roses symbolize the powers that be. The ruling elite or royalty. It is the cross of material life of the four elements. The red symbolizing desires of the material and the lilies purity or spirit. In the ruling factions this is the lily or fleur-de-lis symbol connected to the clubs suit (wands) which is the clover or trefoil. Fleur-de-lis is associated with divine rulership by mythological gods in the forms of serpents, felines and birds, associated with the tree of life, its forbidden fruit and a trinity of creator gods.

Three of Wands

Taking a trip. A person not from the area. Paying close attention to your business activities or opportunities. Established strength. Commerce. Waiting for things to come.

Symbolism: The spice ships delivering goods. Where sea meets shore. The red coat is earthly desires.

Four of Wands

Joining forces. Power in numbers. Successful in a quest or venture. Creating a blueprint of an idea for the future.

Symbolism: Jewish Chuppah shown in the foreground which represents the couple's future home. Used in an engagement or marriage ceremony. Marriage of the bloodlines. Hybrids. Blue garment with red.

Five of Wands

Building an empire. Building a home or structure. The beginning stages of construction. Joining ideas together.
Symbolism: Sides in a war. Ruling factions and the pieces they own in the world.

Six of Wands

Marriage or committed relationship. Marriage procession or preparation. Winning a business proposal. Support from others.

Symbolism: The king's courier. The laurel wreaths two signs of victory.

Seven of Wands

Struggling. On a road to recovery. Rebuilding in a new direction. Enemies unable to reach you. Valor. Having the higher ground or advantage.

Symbolism: The six against the one. Coming to the mountain of the soul. Attempt to take the soul.

Eight of Wands

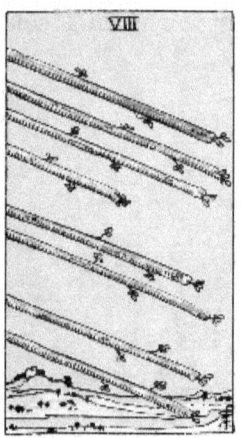

Something is out of balance. Things moving backward. Business or ventures frozen in time. Changing direction. Moving through the immovable.

Symbolism: The life passing through the reincarnation cycle. Time and its control over the soul. Frozen in time.

Nine of Wands

A wall or block. Someone controlling your ability to move forward. Willing to fight for what is yours.

Symbolism: The one eye of the serpent gods. Battling over the karma lords. False prisons.

Ten of Wands

Rebuilding your life. Wearing too many hats. Great physical strength.

Symbolism: The reversed or mirrored world. The harm associated with letting in the angel of death magnified times ten.

Page of Wands

(Pages usually mean a message or a child but here are general meanings.) Holding strong to your beliefs or vision. Someone who looks to the future. Someone who can make their mark on the world. Proclamation.

Symbolism: Mercury, communication from the gods. Second son of the ruler. The red feather is Osiris cult.

Knight of Wands

(Knights usually represent a young adult or situation.) A brave and charismatic person. Time traveler. Gaining control of a fiery situation.

Symbolism: Son of a ruling class bloodline. Heir to the crown. Salamanders on his gold garment are the fire element and the serpent god of the trefoil. The red horse of the 4 horsemen of the apocalypse. The red plumage is Osiris cult.

Queen of Wands

A person who waits on no one. A person who makes their own rules. A soft-hearted generous personality.

Symbolism: The lions the ruling bloodlines of feline head faction of the trefoil. Sunflower and gold garment symbolizing the Sun god. Egyptian lioness goddess Bastet represented here who would sometimes take the form of a household cat, a gentle protector of women and the home. She is an aspect of the triple goddess of Bastet, Sekhmet and Hathor as seen in the Queen of Swords and Empress cards. Bastet is the protector of the home, fire, dance, music, pleasure, sexuality and health.

King of Wands

Someone willing to step outside the box or see another person's opinion/viewpoint. Someone poised and ready at all times to take action. Highly motivated and interactive.

Symbolism: Salamanders on his cape and throne are the fire element and connected to the feline serpent goddess of the trefoil. Red garment is blood and desire. The consort of Bastet the Queen of Wands, he is an aspect of the god Ptah of creation, architecture and craftmanship which is shown in the suit of wands creative energy. The aspect of the creator in Earth. The King of Swords is another aspect.

CHAPTER 20

Additional Keywords & Symbology for the Pentacles Suit

I n my first book I discussed programming your deck. One way of doing this is giving assigned meanings to the cards using keywords or phrases. This helps you remember the card, without having to use a reference booklet. I listed several key words to choose from in that book. Here are some *alternative* meanings to add to those but as always, use what resonates with you.

Here are the meanings for the pentacle cards:

Ace of Pentacles

Really large chunk of money or big opportunity. Gold. Fairies and nature spirits helping. Seeing into or passage through a portal or dimension.

Symbolism: A gift of material ease or gold from the gods. The lilies and roses symbolizing again the material and spiritual. A doorway through or out of time to the soul. It is interesting to note, the pentacle or five-pointed star enclosed in a circle is a sign of man and is an ancient symbol that represents humans' mastery over all inferior beings. Humans are the superior beings. The archway is a portal or initiation and may be connected to the freemasonry degree of The Royal Arch initiation. The Easter lilies are a masonic symbol.

Two of Pentacles

Topsy turvy finances, repeating karmic cycles.

Symbolism: The sideways eight of karma, reincarnation cycle, the gods controlling the cycles. The control of time. Past and future repeating through eons of time. Phallic hat the worship of the masculine god of intelligence. Soul trap of the gods. The anchor symbol is used in freemasonry to ground a ship. We see two ships in the background in turbulent water.

Three of Pentacles

Mastery. Finishing your education/getting a degree. Joining a cult or mind control group. The deed to a house. Monastery.

Symbolism: Aristocracy. Masons. The trefoil of gold coins connected to the Sun God. Pillar underneath the chalice. The Royal Arch Mason of the 3 degrees. A tabernacle is prepared. See the 7 of Swords for the Tabernacle (where sacrifices took place). It is interesting that as I researched the Royal Arch, Waite's name came up (creator of the Rider Waite tarot deck pictured here). "It is regrettable that Masonic research during recent years has failed to throw light upon the origin and early history of the Royal Arch." Arthur Edward Waite, 1921. So, I am definitely on to something. The two figures on the ground are a Catholic Franciscan brother of the third order of Saint Francis of friars and a person wearing a cloak with a hood similar to the boy in the 6 of Cups. This cloak has undecipherable symbols repeated on it. I think this is representing a freemason of the third degree Royal Arch. Talking to the man on the bench wearing an apron that reminds me of the Freemason apron and is cutting stone. The rose symbol carved into the pillar solidifies the Rosicrucian connection and how all of these orders are connected to each other. There are fleur-de-lis symbols next to each pentacle and a symbol for the Earth in the center, divided into the four factions. This is the royal bloodlines that rule different areas of the Earth. The plan that the freemason is holding – which must be a male – has an image of the arch on it. The Royal Arch is connected to a secret ritual. The darkness of the black background suggests the unknown and hidden. The symbol for the Royal Arch is similar to the satanic cross which includes the three lines with the sideways figure eight.

Four of Pentacles

Having energy attachments. Good karma coming to you. You reap what you sow, get what you give.

Symbolism: The kings control the money/gold. This man is wearing a crown which signifies a deity. Possibly Re the Egyptian sun god whose name meant "the mountain of gold". But as we see with the Ace, pentacles represent humans. Rule over humans and controlling their power/true sovereignty. Making the god of humankind money and gold and the seeking of it, as represented by the unnatural cityscape in the background.

Five of Pentacles

Contemplating bankruptcy, looming debt, homelessness. Money or accounts are frozen.

Unforeseen blessings coming. Circumstances changing.

Symbolism: The gods and churches hold the mountain of gold, while humanity is left out in the cold. The stained-glass window was thought to be used in ancient Egypt as they were most likely the creators of glass. The colored beads were used for specific purposes and adorn places of worship. This is shown in the 4 of Swords card as well.

Six of Pentacles

Money needing to be paid out. Taxes or tax return. Someone judging your worth. Meting out justice.

Symbolism: Doubling the three of trinity. The scales are karmic justice. Royalty keeping the spoils and giving very little to the common people. Red coat of material desires. The looped red sash around his waist is a version of an amulet and symbolizes the protection of the female deities. Anubis and other gods/goddesses wear this as well as kings. It symbolizes protective power. The blue, white and red attire may be referencing masonic symbology. The red sash is also linked to the Catholic stole and sash of freemasons.

Seven of Pentacles

Investing money, having back-up money, recognizing value in something.

Symbolism: Here we see grapes being grown for wine in ceremonial rites of ancient Egypt. They were seen as a symbol of resurrection and the transfiguration of kings waiting to traverse to the afterlife. The soul of man on the vine. Wine in ancient Egypt was consumed only by the upper classes and royal family. It was offered up in daily temple rituals in funerary offerings and used in healing. It represented blood and the blood of man or human. Bloodlines. And sacrifice. The Catholic chalice of Christ's blood mirrors this. This could be a nod to the ancient Egyptian God (and Bacchus and others who followed) Shesmu a demon god of the underworld and of the winepress, precious embalming oils and slaughterer of the damned. He is the god of execution throwing the head of a wrongdoer into a winepress to squeeze out the blood as if it was grape juice.

Eight of Pentacles

Apprenticeship. Printing press, publishing, writing books. Money grows on trees for you. Many opportunities, donors or investors.

Symbolism: A mason carving stone. The pillar holding the pentacles represents a sacred science that was known but now is secret and is now encoded into many cathedrals worldwide. If the pentacles represent the human, he is involved in this hidden science. A cedar tree, which this pillar like image could be, is a sign of eternity.

Nine of Pentacles

Extremely privileged or blessed. Having support and back-up. Talking with spirit or with animals, animal communicator. Receiving an important message.

Symbolism: The lady is holding a falcon which represents the Egyptian god Horus, or "Eye of Horus" and considered the king of the air gods. Many other later gods were attributed to Horus. The falcon hooded ties into rituals but we can take this to mean the promise of new life and victory is about to materialize. This woman lives in a stately home as seen in the background behind the falcon. It has a castle turret which would suggest royalty.

Ten of Pentacles

Working in a factory. Successful industry. Good pay. A family business that you inherit. Transfer of money or real estate coming to you or transfer of a business.

Symbolism: There is a lot going on in this card. Starting with the two tapestries above the elderly gentleman's head, one has a castle on it, with the two towers suggesting the tabernacle symbolism and other references to the towers made with other cards. The black and white checkered border of another larger tapestry suggests the black and white tile floor of the checkerboard of the masons and found in the Temple of Solomon. The lower one has the scales of justice and karma. Scales were used to weigh souls and judgment, but this also refers to notes on a harmonic scale of sound that are not heard by the human ear. Sound that can create or destroy as a tech or tool. There is also a castle motif behind the gentleman. And in the background we see what is an elaborate estate and castle, with the turrets visible over the woman's shoulder and a tower, as depicted in the tower card where money and power can be the downfall. This image suggests bloodlines of royalty who own the gold. The old man is dressed in a robe with specific symbols on it that look like another version of the Royal Arch as mentioned in the 3 of Pentacles and 7 of Pentacles. And the couple and child are standing under an arch (and another symbol I will not mention here). So, this feels like a higher degree of initiation into the order that will continue through the family line. The grapes on the robe also refer to the King of Pentacles and 7 of Pentacles. See those cards for more information. It goes along with the symbols I choose not to explain. There is a nod to the god Anubis again indirectly through the scales and overtly through the two dogs. Anubis uses the scales to judge the soul. The husband in the image is holding a wand. It represents the architect gods and is the serpent wand or Serpent Grail, the Holy Grail and Philosopher's Stone in alchemy. It represents the Spear of Destiny. The true Spear of Destiny may have been a structure or device that could open star gates or gateways. It is resting along the edge of the stone archway here. The flowers in the woman's hair suggest glory, power and victory over death of the family. This card relates to the Moon, Justice, 3 of Pentacles, 9 of Pentacles, King of Pentacles, High Priestess and many other cards in the deck.

Page of Pentacles

(Pages usually mean a message or a child but here are general meanings.) Being given a gift or donation. Bringing an idea into the practical or real world. Sharing practical knowledge with the world. Letting go of money's hold on you.

Symbolism: The red hat can be the desire for money, and the green garment envy. But this card has deeper meanings. The red hat and scarf suggest progeny in an order or bloodline. It is blood, sacrifice, struggle, heroism, charity and devotion to the order and bloodline.

Knight of Pentacles

(Knights usually represent a young adult or situation.) A practical young man/woman who is committed and wants to start a business or family. Looking toward the future. Seeing the potential and confident it will pay off.

Symbolism: The black horse of the four horsemen of the apocalypse of famine. This is also the aspect of the Mars god as guardian of agriculture who is connected to the other aspects shown in the Knight of Swords and Emperor, as the god of war. He is armored for battle yet planting a field. This is the spiritual battle for souls. A black horse is a symbol of death and dark forces and can be connected to black magic and mind control. It also represents the strength of maturity to handle what life brings. The dark horse was a messenger of esoteric knowledge and the keeper of secrets and mysteries. In the cults and orders of modern day that trace back to the Egyptian pharaoh bloodlines, the dark horse is the death horse. The Anti-Christ – false messiah – being welcomed in by Illuminati and other orders such as Skull and Bones etc. to build his empire, using black magic and mind control to defeat the Christ. Red soil in the image and the Pentacle, the blood of souls. This card and the Queen of Pentacles has a connection to Memphis. The acacia tree leaves coming from his helmet are connected to freemasonry – see Queen of Pentacles. A sprig of acacia tree represents immortality and resurrection and is an initiation of a 3rd degree mason. It is speculated that Jesus wore a crown of acacia thorns which represented sacrifice and rebirth.

Queen of Pentacles

The birth of a well-funded business. Being born into money. Generous. Valuing money above all else. Gold digger. Someone who appreciates the value of money.

Symbolism: Beginning with her crown, this signifies a deity. The wings on the top relate to the Queen of Cups card related to the Ark of the Covenant. On the throne you see the goat god, and an image of Pan on the side. This could also be seen as earth elementals or gnomes. The rabbit or hare in the foreground symbolizes "to open" or open one's eyes to the mysteries. The mountains, even though part of the topography are a masonic symbol. Red cloak with white. Headdress veil. There are pears on her throne which represent a gift of the gods and femininity. Roses at top represent worldly desires. Pan is seen on the side of the throne as the god of sexuality and fertility as well as the rabbit. Letters are visible in the blown-up Rider Waite deck on the edge of her throne. Possible LISOS or LISGS? Not sure what those represent. If you have information on it, please message me. The Acacia tree is connected to this card as well with the mountainous terrain and roses above her. Acacia is a sacred wood commonly called "shittah" which is utilized in the making of furniture and other items especially put together for the Ark of the Covenant and the Sacred Tabernacle of God. Heredom is a word meaning "high-degree" in Freemasonry from the French Rose Croix rituals, referring to a mythical mountain in Scotland. Royalty from the bloodlines usually live in mountainous places.

ANMARIE UBER

King of Pentacles

Ideas and ventures flourish under this person. Teaching the ropes to apprentices. A person of sound financial advice. Big corporation or famous person. Leader in industry.

Symbolism: Here is the deity crowned of the god Apis, the bull. He is one aspect of the god head of Ptah and Osiris. The armored leg is a connection to The Emperor. We see roses and lilies in several of the cards. They are represented here on his crown, the lilies replaced with the fleur-de-lis of the ruling families. This is divine rulership and depicting a deity with the crown. The scepter with the world on top is ruling the world. The Pentacle is ruling over man. The castle in the background is where the ancient families of pharaohs still live and rule. The red and blue roof another nod to ancient Egypt and freemasons. The grape vines on his coat and growing around him relate back to the 7 of Pentacles card. Wine and blood sacrifice.

CHAPTER 21

Running a Professional Business

Running your own tarot reading business is an excellent idea, as it can be done full or part time, and does not require a huge investment. Plus, it helps people, so let's get into this.

I am not a lawyer, and do not pretend to give legal advice. The following information in this chapter is suggestions from my own experience and in response to those who have asked.

SETTING UP YOUR BUSINESS

There are many ways to run a tarot business. You can do readings in person, work psychic fairs, do private parties, read online, read for a psychic hotline, open your own new age store, take donations on social media for live readings or work out of a place of business. You could even build up your business and hire other readers. The ideas and opportunities are endless. However, there is a lot of competition and you need to set yourself apart. The best way to do this is to read accurately. A high quality accurate and uplifting reading is hard to find these days. Another way to set yourself apart would be to focus on a niche. Maybe you read with a deck of ordinary playing cards (of which there would be no Major Arcana). Maybe you read with your own deck that you designed. Maybe you focus on a certain group of people that you read for, such as Star Seeds, special relationships, Soul Path readings etc. Choose something you are interested in that makes you stand out.

Depending on how and where you choose to read, there are a lot of things to consider when running your own business. Is it going to be an actual business, or are you going to run it like a profitable hobby?

As you get busy you may need to think about getting a website and a way to take payments, such as Paypal or Stripe. This could be a shopping cart or simply a button on your website page. And literally, these days all you need is a page. If you decide to get scheduling software (saves a lot of work and headaches scheduling people, confirming and taking payments) they can take the payments for you and notify the client. They also handle workshops, refunds and a number of other small tasks so you don't have to.

Another option is reading on a psychic call site. While you will still most likely have to pay your own taxes, they will do the marketing and scheduling for you.

Maybe you want to hire psychics. If you are going to have employees, you will need an EIN number (in the USA). Sometimes this is good to have anyway even if you work alone, so you do not have to use your social security number anywhere. You will have to look at all the local laws involved with having employees.

Or having 1099 employees, which means they are independent contractors. So, go as big or small as you want.

Another important factor when working as a psychic, are legal issues connected to the advice you give clients. In the United States, being a tarot reader is considered "for entertainment purposes only". This is why it is important to get a disclaimer on your website or have in-person clients sign a form of agreement that states clearly that your readings do not replace the advice of legal counsel, medical advice, or any other professional is a good idea. If a client is suicidal or needs professional counseling, have resources or suggestions handy for them to contact. You should never take responsibility for someone's emotional, mental or physical state by putting yourself in the role of saving them. This is outside your scope of legal permissions in most countries. You can however lead the person in a more positive direction and be honest with them (*how honest* I will talk about in a bit). You are not able to offer legal counseling. If you have a doctorate in Divinity, you may be legally allowed to offer spiritual counsel. If you hold a degree in a specialized area, obviously that is a different story. You would have to check into the local laws in your area to find out what you can and cannot do.

Consulting a lawyer is always a good idea before starting any business.

CHOOSING A LUCKY BUSINESS NAME

You may want to consider choosing a name that is in harmony with Chaldean Numerology, and will bring in good karma/success, as well as picking the best launch day. A crash course can be found on my website: "Cheatsheet: How to name your business using Chaldean Numerology". It is also available on retailers for .99. However, there is a bit of finagling that happens when doing this process, so I recommend learning the whole number system, or having me check your name and launch day.

BECOMING WHAT YOU PROMOTE

Being in a position of influence means you should have worked on your own issues and be on the path of finding truth – which means searching for truth, being unafraid to face truth when it comes, questioning what you are told, and continuing to seek. The more you uncover, awaken and remember (this has nothing to do with channeling which is relying on an outside being to drip "truth" to you – most if not all are very sophisticated deceivers with agendas - but rather getting in touch with your own soul) the more you can help, guide and inspire others. Remove fear and the entity or being that is keeping it in your consciousness. The more you teach others to go within, the more people you help.

THE IMPORTANCE OF ETHICS

Readings are ALWAYS confidential. You are not held to any law that says you cannot tell someone else about a reading. But ethics say you should keep everything that happens confidential. I treat my business as I do my massage business. I am under the health board and prevented from telling anyone, even another family member that a client received a massage with me. The visit itself is confidential. If they ask me if "so-and-so" liked their massage, I can only respond with something like, "I am not at liberty to discuss whether _____ is a client of mine." I would suggest you use this same practice.

You can however give examples of sessions and share experiences, as long as no names or locations are used, or any obvious and specific details that would clearly point to a certain individual. Readings on celebrities, and those in the public eye are okay to share, as long as you only use information that is available publicly and link it clearly to "conjecture". Digging into someone's personal affairs is only going to bring you trouble.

THE IMPORTANCE OF DETACHING FROM A CLIENT

When giving a tarot reading, in most cases you will be using psychic/intuitive faculties (although I do teach you how to read cards with no intuition and still be accurate, which is an option) that enrich the meanings of the cards. But before you offer readings to anyone, I would like you to analyze the *way* you read. It is my belief you should not be in someone's energy at all. You should be able to read for them, with only a first name, no visual... nothing else to go on, other than your intention for information. This means you are reading purely from soul, and do not need any physical contact with the person. You do not need to know what they look like. If you can do this, then the chances are good that you are not doing any of the following things you need to worry about.

It is important that you are not psychically hooking your energy into the other person. You need to be concerned for them, but not responsible. You should not be trying to read their mind or entering their energy field in any way. Even though this can give you access to extremely detailed information about the person - which may seem helpful to establishing trust with the client - the reasons you want to avoid this practice are:

1. You can take on their energy and anything else in their energy field – the bad and the good, including attachments.

2. The customer often figures out something is wrong, or that you have hooked in, or interfered with their energy. Usually after 1 – 3 visits and will go to someone else. They will be especially angry if they have to pay an energy worker to get your energy removed.

3. You will lead the client only on one path – the path they are

currently on - instead of helping them see other options. This is because you are reading their current mindset and decisions.

4. Because of number three, your advice tends to be bad advice in many cases, because they weren't presented with other options. And if they act on your advice, and it goes south, this will them to go elsewhere for readings.

5. You limit the reading from being much more profound and going in directions the client never dreamed of visiting. Soul information is so much more encompassing than mind or energy body. The client will feel a sense of rightness, natural empowerment and upliftment. As if they have reconnected with themselves and rebalanced.

6. And finally, it is unethical. In my opinion, entering another person's energy, thoughts and private business affairs is an invasion. If you are unconsciously doing this, it is time to reexamine your process.

THE IMPORTANCE OF NOT BEING JUDGEY

Your personal beliefs about how someone should or should not live their life have no place in a reading. People have their own lives, religious beliefs, challenges and you haven't walked in their shoes.

One example is I overheard another reader say to a client was, "That is a sin." She was referencing this girl's decision to have sex before marriage. The reader actually brought her religious beliefs into the session and imposed them on this girl, shaming her. Or let's say someone is wanting out of a marriage, and they are already involved with someone else. If you have personal issues with cheating, or believe that marriage is sacred, remember that this is their life, and not your place to judge. You are there to answer their questions, which will probably run along the lines of "will this new person be a good partner for me", "make me happy", etc. Since they are jumping into something new, before they are even out of the old relationship, you may want to look at the new partner and question if they are going to be similar to the person they married and will have the same issues to deal with. Or maybe the reading leads to questions about whether their spouse will let them out of the marriage easily? Or maybe the children are still holding them there. Does the marriage have any hope of recovering? And so on.

PREPARING THE CLIENT FOR A READING - WHAT TO EXPECT

Here is what I tell clients prior to a reading, even if they have had one before.

- The cards are just a visualization tool and have no power of their own. All things can be used for the good.
- I explain that they should feel better after their reading and receive several confirmations for what they already know. (If you feel worse after a reading, the person either didn't give you all your options, and/or failed to show you something positive beyond any negative predictions. Basically, they took away your power to change anything or told you something too early that you weren't ready to hear...or the worst...told you something that wasn't even accurate or a worst-case scenario.) It is okay to tell people unpleasant things. In fact, it is better to be truthful than tell people what you think they want to hear. A lot of times you will find they are already aware of it through their own intuition. But I feel it is imperative to leave the session on a positive note, and empower the client to change their situation, if possible.
- To change a situation, I explain that there are almost always multiple choice options in any given scenario. You may be on Path A, but Path B or C might be

better outcomes. If you don't give a client the other options on their path, they will continue down Path A and miss choosing a better scenario they didn't know about and that you didn't look for. This irritates me to no end with psychics who read for me and just give me one script. It means they are just reading me and my energy and thoughts/emotions which are causing my current condition, and not giving me tools to change that and see another path. Even if you can't change something negative like getting fired, you can usually do something different in the interim to lessen the effects or perceive the event differently. For example, in a reading you tell a client who is asking about their job that you see them getting fired. (This should not be said to a client until you have FIRST looked to see if there is something they could do to change that such as altering their behavior at work, talking to the boss etc. Hearing that you are about to be fired – or any bad news - can be shocking and devastating. And you should always remember that other people are involved and could change their mind. So, you want to make sure that you are looking in the present moment, and in that future moment.) If it is looking like getting fired is a sure thing, and nothing can change it, then you should immediately be looking to the future to see if this is a blessing in disguise and something better is coming along etc.

- And finally, if something I say doesn't resonate, just leave it behind. And realize that things can change, just by getting the reading and becoming aware of them.

END OF CHAPTER ACTIVITY

1. Think about why you want to start a business. Is it to get out of a day job? Bring in more money for your child's needs? Do you love doing readings or interacting with the public one-on-one?
2. What is your special niche or ability with card reading?
3. Research owning your own business, if you have never done it before. Will this be just a hobby or side-gig?
4. Take the first steps today to set up your business.

CHAPTER 22
Conclusion

Dear Reader,

Have confidence in yourself. Have confidence in your intuition. It is never wrong. Practice makes better. Better makes even better. Keep going. This is a journey. The truth will come. But most of all, help and inspire people. Lift them up. *Always* leave a reading on a positive note with hope or good news. *Always.* There are *always* options or different choices. *Always.*

It is time for all of us to flourish. To become the Abundant Sovereign Souls that we are, and step into our purpose.

Thank you for all your love and support over the years,

Anmarie

If you enjoyed this book, please consider leaving a review.

Bibliography

Freemasonscommunity.life

Egyptian-gods.org

About the Author

Anmarie Uber's interest in the metaphysical field has continued, throughout most of her life. She had her first remembered contact with the other side, at age three, and an insatiable passion, throughout childhood, for ghosts, UFOs and anything paranormal. Anmarie began exploring astrology and numerology at age 16, and tarot, yoga, massage, nutrition, palmistry, crystal healing, Feng Shui, energy healing, and the philosophy of reincarnation at age 21. Her ongoing quest for spiritual truth has been all-consuming, and has many times taken precedence over personal needs, or worldly goals. What she has found, is that many "new age" belief systems, can be roads to nowhere...another program to be sifted through. Although Anmarie has studied and lived countless spiritual and religious ideologies, the last five years of her life have been the most challenging, as the pressure to keep humanity down is increasing. Anmarie believes in finding the humor in difficult situations, forgiving hardships and lessons with others, and having faith. We are all programmed beings, trying to awaken...and awakening to your true Self, is the most important accomplishment in life.

Also by Anmarie Uber

60 Second Tarot
Signs of a Soulmate
5 Numbers of Destiny
Number Code
Breaking your Magnetic Patterns
Recreate your Identity
Synchronicity Numbers
Nature Talk

www.ingramcontent.com/pod-product-compliance
Lightning Source LLC
Chambersburg PA
CBHW070545010526
44118CB00012B/1222